Buy Homes Not Shoes (Or Other Stuff)

A Women's Guide to Buying Her First Home

Tamara Celeste

ISBN: 978-1-7323775-0-9

Free Gift for My Readers

As a way of saying "Thank You" to my Readers, I have a special gift for you. I want to send you my free guide *"8 Common Mistakes First Time Homebuyers Make and How to Avoid Them."*

Get your copy by visiting the link below.
https://tamaraceleste.com/8-common-mistakes

Special Bonus for My Readers

As another way of saying "Thank You" to my Readers, please click on the link below and you will receive my free 1-Page Downloadable Cheat Sheet *"50 Quick Home Buying Tips, To Save You Time & Money"*.

Get your copy by visiting the link below.
https://tamaraceleste.com/50-quick-homebuying-tips

Table of Contents

Introduction

"The best advice I ever got was that knowledge is power and to keep reading"

~ David Bailey

Do me a favor and put down this book for a minute and go look in your closet. That's right: I said go look in your closet. What do you see? How many pairs of shoes do you have? How many are still in the boxes that you haven't yet worn? How many clothes still have tags on them? A recent article states that "50% of women claim 25% of their wardrobe sits in the closet collecting dust. A whopping 73% of women update 25% of their closet every 3 months."[1]

We live in a society where things and the accumulation of things are so valued. Designer labels and the car you drive are valued even more. Even if someone can't afford the labels *per se,* they will chase the fantasy by spending money and accumulating debt on items (clothes, bags, shoes) they can't afford. Some even think that because they are putting it on the credit card and paying the monthly minimum that it means they can afford what they are buying. But even if you can afford it, ask yourself this: do you really need all of that stuff like clothes, shoes, bags, and dinners out 2 – 4 times a week? Or would that money be better spent paying down debt, investing and saving for the future?

---

[1] Kim P, (November 15th, 2017) *Average Cost of Clothing Per Month Will Surprise You* [Credit Donkey™]

In one of my favorite shows of all time, *Sex in the City*, there is a scene where Carrie Bradshaw (played by Sarah Jessica Parker) needs to buy the apartment she lives in from her ex-boyfriend. She has no assets and very little savings. She is, ironically, sitting in a shoe store with her friend Miranda when she asks herself: "Where did all of my money go? I know I made some!" Miranda then points out to her that she has about 100 pairs of shoes; at $400 a pop that was her down payment of $40,000. Well, by this point Carrie is beside herself. She says to herself, "I spent $40,000 on shoes and I have no place to live? I literally will be the old woman that lives in her shoes."

Don't get me wrong, I was that girl who loved to shop. I remember during my first internship in college, I was living at home, working in the legal department at a major insurance company and I was making $15 an hour. In the early 90's that was a lot of money. I remember one of my colleagues at work asking me, "How does a college student have so many business suits?" In my young adult mind, I had to spend money looking good in order to leave a good impression. When I graduated from law school and finally began to make a regular, steady salary, I shopped every weekend. Suits, sweaters, shoes, boots, (oh, how I love boots!) bags, anything I could get my hands on. I justified it because I usually bought everything on sale. My family used to say that I "got it honest" from my grandmother, God rest her soul.

My maternal grandmother, Minnie, was a spendthrift. She always looked good and had new clothes every season and for any reason. Her hair and nails were always done and she had a new car every few years. This was the 1970's, and my grandmother was an independent woman. She was a social worker, so she always had her own money and didn't rely on my grandfather or have to get his "permission" to support her spending habits. I admired my grandmother as a little girl and I didn't realize just how independent she was until I got older and it made me admire and appreciate her and her accomplishments even more.

I used to take the "getting it honest" remark, comparing me to her, as a compliment and laugh it off. But one day, several years later, I looked in my closet and all of the "things" I had acquired and decided enough was enough. It was time for me to grow up, to woman up and start by buying my first home and subsequently begin investing in real estate.

Again, I want to ask you: when you look at your closet what do you see? Or pull out our credit card statements for the past year and see where you have spent your money; we all have our unique obsessions. Maybe it's shoes, maybe it's clothes, maybe it's expensive sneakers for your children, maybe it's expensive housewares, travelling, jewelry, etc. It's important to really look at what could have been a down payment on your new condo, townhome or house? Or maybe it's the car you drive. Because of the monthly payment, maintenance and insurance, it leaves you with little to no extra money to save.

I recently received a call from an acquaintance saying she is ready to purchase a home. I worked with some of her family members in the past and we have kept in touch over the last couple of years. I was excited when she called to say she was finally ready to purchase her home. Now, this young lady, who I will call Michelle, has great credit and very good income, so when we first started talking I thought she would be a slam dunk for getting approved for a mortgage. But guess what? Her car recently died, so she had to purchase a new car. She didn't purchase just any car, she purchased her dream car. It was a new Mercedes and the car payment alone was about the same as a mortgage on a new home. What did this "dream" purchase cost her? A new home! Right now, she could only get approved for a small mortgage because she was carrying too much debt with the new car. I asked Michelle if she considered trading in the car for a less expensive car so that she would be able to qualify for a larger mortgage loan. She admitted that the car depreciated[2], as soon as she drove it off the lot. As a result, she knew she was upside down, meaning she owed more than what the car is worth. If she sold it or traded it in she would have to pay too much out of her pocket to pay off the car loan.

Here's the moral to the story:

1. Don't bite off more than you can chew; don't spend above your means. Yes, you may be able to technically "afford: something, but just because you can, doesn't mean you should. Spending to the top of your limit takes away other choices you have on where you can invest your money.

2. Don't spend top dollar for a big-ticket item like a car that will depreciate, until you own at least one appreciating[3] asset[4] like real estate.

Okay, perhaps none of the above applies to you and you don't spend a lot of money on "things that depreciate." Perhaps you have thought about buying a home, however you simply

---

[2] When something depreciates, it loses value over time or as it ages.
[3] When something appreciates, it increases in value over time.
[4] An asset is something of value, an asset can appreciate (such as a house or antiques), or depreciate (such as a car).

don't know where to begin. You have questions about how much money is required or where to start the process.

This book is about helping you get from where you are now (Point A) to where you desire to be (Point B.) Everyone reading this book is in a different place in their lives, so getting from point A for you could be learning the basic steps to purchasing a home, or figuring out how much you should save, or what your credit score should be. While for someone else, Point A could be finding a Realtor® or a mortgage lender. Just know that no matter where you are in the process, my goal is to support you exactly where you are.

I would like to take a moment to congratulate you and acknowledge you for your commitment to home ownership. I also want to thank you for putting your trust in me and this book. There are hundreds (probably thousands) of books about buying a home, but I wanted to create a book just for you! That's right, YOU: the woman reading this right now. I have to say that I am super excited to be on this journey with you.

Before we go any further, I want to share with you a little bit about myself...

I was a quiet introverted child. Only kidding! That was so not me! Let me start over. I was born and raised in Hartford, Connecticut; when I was about nine years old my grandfather, Arthur, who only had an 8th grade education, gave me a choice. He said, "When you grow up you can either be a doctor, a lawyer, or a pharmacist." After this conversation, I literally grew up thinking that those where my only three options in life. On one hand, this was a good thing because I know my grandfather's intentions were in the right place. But on the other hand, it was a bad thing because I never explored any other career options. When I got to high school and realized that science was just not my thing, along with the fact that whenever I walked into a hospital just the smell alone made me want to faint. I went to my grandfather, remember I really only thought I had three career options, and said this, "I don't like science and can't stand the sight of blood, so I guess I have to be a lawyer. "

My family was by no means wealthy, not even close, but never once did money come up as a deterrent to me achieving my goal of becoming a lawyer. No one ever asked me how I was going to pay for college and law school or tried to dissuade me. Once I said I was going to be a lawyer everyone in my family fell in line with it and said Tami (that's what my family calls me) is going to be a lawyer. Looking back, I am truly grateful to my family for the confidence and encouragement they gave me as a child, I grew up believing I could accomplish anything (as long as I became a lawyer first).

A year after graduating from Northeastern University, in Boston, I left the cold for warmer weather, and much more humid climate, and enrolled in law school at Loyola University in New Orleans. After graduating from law school, I worked at two law firms in Louisiana and then went to work on Wall Street at Solomon Brothers, and then subsequently I went to work at Goldman Sachs. While I was working at Goldman Sachs I purchased my first condo and purchased several investment properties.

I then decided it was time to leave my job to launch my dream business, which was, get this, a shoe line for women with large feet. How ironic, given the title of this book! I ran it for several years and it eventually dissolved (more about that later).

When I moved to Florida, I wanted a different career. I decided to get my real estate license and never looked back. If someone would have told me 20 years ago that I would be selling homes for a living, I would have thought they were out of their minds. My plan was to retire from corporate America or open my own law firm, but be a Realtor®? Well, like the saying goes, if you want to hear God laugh tell *her* your plans.

My real estate career has been more satisfying than I could have ever imagined. I have helped thousands of people, and in the process, I have gained so much from working with them. I have grown professionally in more ways than I can describe. In my current career is where I found my passion and my calling. It is not about the sale for me, it's about my client's and walking them through entire home buying process. When I am working with my clients, especially the ones that are first time home buyers, I really enjoy educating them so that they feel informed and secure in their decision to purchase a home. I just LOVE it when we are at the end of the closing and it's time for them to get their keys, seeing the excitement on their faces and the sense of accomplishment in their eyes. Those moments are priceless.

What I have realized over the more than a decade of helping my clients purchase homes is that many of the same questions, concerns, and fears are expressed over and over again. I realize, just like with anything, you don't know what you don't know. If you have never purchased a home before how would you know the difference between a down payment and closing costs? Or how would you know that a home warranty protection plan can save you thousands of dollars in repair costs in the long run? You won't. That's why I wrote this book. I want you to be informed and educated so that you know the right questions to ask and, also so that you can feel both comfortable and confident in taking the next step toward homeownership.

I want to offer this advice to you: Buying your first home is a journey. Take your time. Trust yourself and your instincts. You will know when something feels right and when it doesn't.

One thing that I would like to mention up front. Buying a home is exciting, but not everyone is going to be excited for you. There are some people who may not understand why you want to do this and some may actually try to discourage you from achieving your goal. Be careful who you select to be on this journey with you. Recognize when the feedback is or is not coming from a place of love. Your loved ones may fear for you, or they may be projecting their own fears of scarcity on you. Remember, you are under no obligation to share your intention to purchase a home with anyone. You can always tell everyone after your closing when you give them your new address and invite them to your housewarming party!

Here's a perfect example of what I'm referring to: I recently called one of my best friends to ask her if she would be available on a certain weekend. I wanted to visit her and her family in Dallas and to meet my new "niece" (her newborn baby) in person. She left me a message and said, "I got your message, I don't know if that weekend is good, but call me back." When I called her back she explained to me that she and her husband had made an offer to purchase a larger house around the corner from where they currently own a home but they didn't want to tell anyone until they actually purchased their new home.

Now, my friend has owned at least three or four homes over the years since graduating from law school. She and her husband would have no problem getting approved for mortgage. They both have great jobs and great credit, so being rejected for a mortgage was highly unlikely. Yet she still did not want anyone to know. When I asked her why she was keeping this a secret, her response was she and her husband did not feel like fielding questions from relatives as to why they felt the needed to move. They also didn't want to hear things like, "You have so much going on with the baby. Shouldn't you wait to buy another house?" Or, "Do you really think now is a good time to move?" Their family members, of course, had their best interests at heart, but at that moment in time their best interests weren't particularly helpful. My friend and her husband needed to do what was best for them and their family without comments, criticism, or advice from anyone.

That being said, I am not those people. I am excited for you to get started, and I will be here with you, encouraging you every step of the way!

Prologue

"Buying a home should be exciting and easy, not complicated and confusing."

~ *Tamara Celeste*

I am so glad that you are considering purchasing your first home. For most people, purchasing their first home is a big milestone to be celebrated. On the flip side, it is a process that can be emotionally and financially daunting. The terminology can be overwhelming, and talking to your friends and families about their experiences and what to expect often makes you more confused. Amidst this confusion sometimes the obvious is overlooked. You just don't know where to begin.

Additionally, questions come up. Questions like:

- Who do I speak to first, a lender or a Realtor®?

- How much do I save for a down payment?

This book will answer all your questions (and the questions you didn't know that you had.) It will guide you through the process with ease and empower you so that when you are ready to purchase your home, you are informed, confident and ready to move forward towards your dream of homeownership.

Just to clarify, this book should not, I repeat, should NOT be a substitute for a real estate professional, assisting you with your home purchase. In fact, the National Association of Realtors® (NAR) 2017 Home Buyer and Seller Generational Trends Report stated: "All generations of buyers continue to consult a real estate agent or broker to help them buy and sell their homes. Buyers need the help of a real estate professional to help them find the right home"[5] Use this book as a resource and a learning tool and find the right team to assist you with your home buying needs.

---

[5] National Association of Realtors® Research Department, "Home Buyer and Seller Generational Trends Report 2017" p 4
https://www.nar.realtor/sites/default/files/reports/2017/2017-home-buyer-and-seller-generational-trends-03-07-2017.pdf

Benefits of Homeownership

A Profile of Home Buyers and Sellers published by NAR in 2017 found that first-time home buyers made up 34% of all home buyers. 18% of all buyers were single females. The report also noted that 30% of all home buyers stated: "the primary reason for purchasing a home was the desire to own a home of their own."[6]

According to the U.S. Department of Housing and Urban Development, studies have shown that "homeowners accumulate wealth as the investment in their homes grows, enjoy betting living conditions, are often more involved in their communities and have children who tend on average to do better in school and are less likely to become involved with crime.[7]"

Furthermore, a 2015 Habitat for Humanity Report[8] has shown that some of the additional benefits to homeownership include:

Increases in:

- High school graduation rates
- Children's good health
- Net family wealth
- Safety and security

[6] National Association of Realtors®, "2017 Profile of Home Buyers and Seller" 2017, p 6. https://www.nar.realtor/sites/default/files/documents/2017-profile-of-home-buyers-and-sellers-11-20-2017.pdf

[7] Boehm, Dr. Thomas P., Schlottmann, Dr. Alan, Abt. Associates Inc. "Wealth Accumulation and Homeownership Evidence for Low-Income Households" *U.S. Department of Housing and Urban Development Office of Policy Development and Research*, December 2004 *https://www.huduser.gov/portal/Publications/pdf/WealthAccumulationAndHomeownership.pdf*

[8] "Habitat for Humanity, Beneficial impacts of homeownership: A research summary." http://www.habitatbuilds.com/wp-content/uploads/2016/04/Benefits-of-Homeownership-Research-Summary.pdf

Decreases in:

- Children's behavior problems
- Reliance on government assistance
- Doctor visits and health related issues

How is that for added benefits?

This book is divided into nine chapters that touch on everything from mindset and getting in the right headspace, to defining common real estate terms, and much more. There are charts (I love charts!) and some exercises for you to complete that will help you hold yourself accountable and help you to remember the concepts. These exercises will also allow you to jot down your goals so that you will be able to come back and reference your answers as you move forward.

Before we move forward I want to take a moment to be honest and say that sometimes homeownership may not be right for you RIGHT NOW. For example, you may live a city like San Francisco or New York where it may be more cost effective for you to rent than to buy. Or you may be planning to quit your job and go back to school next year and you need to save in order prepare for the reduction in income. In the last chapter of this book I will provide you with some alternatives if any of the above scenarios fit your situation. Regardless of where you are right now, if you feel that at some point in the future homeownership is for you, please continue reading this book. I promise, you won't have any regrets.

Finally, I want to mention that every state (and county) has different real estate laws and customs. This book does not address each state specifically, although I do reference my state of Florida when I give examples. The purpose of this book is to give a general overview of the home buying process. Please consult a local Realtor® for laws and customs specific to you state. For assistance in finding a Realtor® near you please visit: https://tamaraceleste.com/find-a-realtor/

I truly hope that you find value and that you will share your questions and revelations with me at https://www.facebook.com/groups/BuyHomesNotShoes/ where you will be supported and encouraged.

Now get to work!!
Xoxo
Tamara Celeste

CHAPTER 1

Taking Back Your Power
by Taking Control

"The past cannot be changed. The future is yet in your power."

~ Unknown

Have you ever thought what it would it be like if you didn't have to get permission from another person, your Landlord, to paint or do other projects in the house that you wish to do to make it feel more like your home? Have you ever wondered what it would be like if you didn't have to worry year after year when it was time for your lease to be renewed if your landlord was going to raise the rent, or decide not to renew your lease for no reason at all? You would then be forced to uproot yourself and pull together the money for first month's rent, last month's rent and a security deposit for a new place. You would also have additional moving expenses such as truck rental, labor fees, storage costs. Never mind having to leave all those memories behind.

Here is the problem:

The problem when you rent you is that you are not in control of your own destiny. There is a false sense of security when you rent a home. This is because, as we just discussed, your landlord could decide to:

1. Raise the rent

2. Sell their property to a new owner

3. Refuse to renew your lease

The landlord also has access to your property at any time, with notice of course. But even so, where is the security and privacy in this for you or your family?

As I was writing this book a client that I worked with about eight years ago called me and said: "Tamara, I just received a letter from my landlord and he is increasing my rent by $200 next month, can he do that?" Unfortunately, the answer is yes. You see her lease was expiring and the landlord wanted her to sign a lease with the new monthly rental amount which was $200 more than what she was currently paying. Eight years ago my client, who I will call Jodi, was going through a divorce and I sold her home for her as part of the divorce proceedings and since that time she has been renting. When we spoke, she was so upset about the increase that she asked if I thought she could buy a house. As it turned out she had a great credit score, good income and very little debt so we got her approved for a mortgage and now she is looking to purchase her new home and will be paying approximately the same monthly payment as her new rent would have been.

Now is the time to take back control of your future, your life, and, more importantly, to take back control of a basic human need: the need for housing for you and your family.

Describe in detail below how you are going to feel when you purchase your home and take back control.

CHAPTER 2

Myths, Mindset & Minefields

"Infuse your life with action. Don't wait for it to happen.

Make it happen. Make your own future Make your own hope."

~ *Bradley Whitford*

I have worked with and talked to thousands of women over the years. In doing this, I have observed that there are three primary beliefs that women hold that initially impede them from taking action and purchasing a home:

1. They have some preconceived notions (myths) that create barriers to homeownership.

2. They don't believe that homeownership is meant for them.

3. The fear of the unknown causes them to make excuses.

I am here to get you over those mental hurdles. I will break down the process for you into small bite-size chunks so that you can purchase the home that you have been dreaming about.

Myths

First, I want to talk about and dispel the two most common myths that prevent many potential first time homebuyers from even trying because they believe that owning a home is unattainable.

Myth #1
You need "perfect" credit to buy a home.

Fact #1
You don't need perfect credit to buy a home. In fact most people in the US do not have "perfect credit" but you must have fair to good credit. Below are the most important things to note about your credit score:

- You should have a credit score of AT LEAST 600, but the higher the better.

- I've seen people succeed in purchasing a home with a 580-credit score, but that is not the norm and the interest rate was very high.

- The items on your credit report should show that they are current with a good payment history for the past 6 - 12 months.

Myth #2
You need to have a lot of money for a down payment, 20% or more, to buy a home.

Fact #2

You don't need 20% down. The 20% 'rule' comes from the fact that if you have 20% down you don't need to purchase mortgage insurance, which I will explain in chapter 5. Furthermore, "a lot" of money is relative to the individual, it isn't a specific dollar figure. Don't just take someone else's word that you need "a lot" of money to buy a home. In some cases, you can purchase a home with as little as 3% or 3.5% down. What does that translate to? About $3000 - $3500 down for a $100,000 house. Most of you would spend more than that on first and last month's rent and a security deposit when it's time to move into another rental.

We will discuss your credit score and what the down payment is and how it works much more in depth a little later in the book, but I felt that these two points had to be mentioned in the beginning so that we could get them out of the way. Now that we have that cleared up, take a deep breath and relax a little bit. I want you to enjoy this journey knowing that you don't have to be "perfect" to buy a home. If you did, very few people would own a home.

Mindset

One of my favorite coaches and authors T. Harv Eker says in his book Secrets of the Millionaire Mind:

"No thought lives in your head rent-free. Each thought you have will either be an investment or a cost. It will either move you toward happiness and success or away from it. It will either empower you or disempower you. That's why it is important you choose your thoughts and beliefs wisely9."

You have already taken a big step in the right direction by making up your mind to take action! You are about to endeavor upon a journey of not only buying your first home but also building wealth and increasing your net worth through homeownership. Just by buying this book, taking time out of your busy schedule to actually read it, and completing the exercises, you have shown that you are already in the mindset of homeownership.

Whenever you embark on something new, it is inevitable to have a mindset shift. Something in you had to say, I'm ready to make the change. When I was thinking about writing this book, it took me a year to finally sit down and write it. Why? First, I had to find the time, ok -- I'm going to call myself out on this one -- I procrastinated, plain and simple! Second, I had doubts. I had doubts that I wouldn't be able to complete it, I had doubts that no one would want to read it, and that no one would find it worthwhile. Third, I was afraid that people would criticize my efforts and what I was trying to accomplish. But every single one of those thoughts and feelings were fleeting. More importantly, they were not stronger than my desire to make a difference by providing this information in a format that is easy to understand in the hopes that I can add value and help enhance the lives of others.

You have to believe that you are worthy of and entitled to home ownership. You have to believe that you are worthy and entitled to build wealth. You have to believe that even though

---

9 Eker, T . Harv, *Secrets of the Millionaire Mind 2005, p*

you may not have grown up in a home that your parents owned, it doesn't mean that homeownership is not for you and your family. Alternatively, say you did grow up in a home your parents owned, but you feel that you have not accomplished as much as your parents have financially. Maybe you took a slightly different path with your education or career that may not have afforded you the ability to buy a home as early as you would have liked. Whatever you may have thought would keep you from owning a home no longer exists. I want you to commit and declare the following statement out loud daily:

I commit to homeownership. Owning a home is for me!

Even though it may not be an easy process, and you may have to make some sacrifices, with the right attitude and the right knowledge it will be one of the best things you ever do for your current and future self.

Avoid the traps (excuses) that hold you back

I talk to hundreds of people every year. I often meet women that have great jobs, and great income. When I ask them why they don't own a home or why they don't consider buying a home, I hear all kinds of excuses.

One excuse I often hear is, "I make enough and have enough money saved, but I want to wait to buy a home with my future husband." My response to this one is, the operative word here is "future." You can't live in the future, or the past for that matter. You have to focus on the here and now, the present. So I ask this: what is best for you right now? Is purchasing a home best for you right now? It may or may not be. Only you can answer this question. Here's what I did when I was single and purchased my first condo. After I closed on my home I manifested my future husband by leaving a "little" space in the closet for him to hang his clothes!

Another way to look at it is to buy a smaller "starter" home or condo now. Then, when you meet Mr. Right, you can either rent out your starter home or you can sell it. Once you are married, you can take a portion of the profit from your starter home to buy a larger home with your spouse.

Another excuse that I hear quite often is, "I feel comfortable paying my rent but I don't feel comfortable paying a mortgage. What if I lose my job?" I know this is a real concern for many people. Job security is not what it used to be. But let me offer you an alternative way to look at this scenario. You are going to always need a place to live, whether or not you have your current job. You should not live in a state of fear of what may or may not happen, such as losing your job.

Let's say you lost your job tomorrow. Where would you go? What if you owned a home and you lost your job -- could you still go to that place you just named and rent out your home to cover your mortgage and possibly give you a little extra income? Or, could you stay in your home and rent out a room or two through Airbnb (visit www.airbnb.com) or a similar service in order to cover your mortgage? I have a friend who got divorced and was afraid she couldn't afford the home on her own. She decided to try Airbnb. She now makes an extra $2,000.00 - $3,000.00 per month renting out one bedroom in her house to Airbnb travelers. This option may not be for everyone, but these are just options to consider.

One of my all-time favorite excuses is: "I don't want to buy a home until I can get the home that I want." What the heck does that mean? What I have found that people usually mean when they say that is that are suffering from *comparison-itis*. This is when they compare what other people have, to what they think they should have. They want a house like their friend's house even though they can't afford it. Or, even worse, they want to be able to impress their friends, with that "WOW" factor. I'm telling you right now, GET OVER IT! You have to start somewhere. Remember this is your first home. It doesn't have to be your last home. Find what fits in your budget comfortably, something in a neighborhood where you feel safe and that will hopefully increase in value in the future.

I purchased my first condo in the early 2000's. At the time, I was working at Goldman Sachs in downtown Manhattan. Most of my colleagues and friends were in their mid to late twenties or early thirties and we were all living the life, travelling to exotic locations, dining out and having fun in and around Manhattan and the trendy neighborhoods of Brooklyn. But I knew that I wanted to own something, so I started looking for a home. I would have loved to purchase a condo or a co-op in Manhattan or Brooklyn. Although I could have "technically" afforded it at the time, I knew that if I chose to live in New York City, "the life" as I knew it would have come to a screeching halt for me. I would have ended up "house rich and cash poor," which means that my mortgage, condo fees, utilities and other household living expenses would have taken up most of my income and I would be left with little money to spend on anything else. I would have had the bragging rights of having a Manhattan or Brooklyn Heights zip code, but I would have been sitting at home alone on the weekends eating PB&J and watching Sex & The City. I would not have been able to afford to do anything else but pay my mortgage and the bills associated with my new home.

Instead, I ended up finding a "cute and cozy" (real estate lingo for "small") two-bedroom, 700 square foot condo, (yes I said 700 square feet), in downtown Jersey City. It was just two train stops from Manhattan or a quick ferry ride across the Hudson River, which separated New York and New Jersey. I was comfortable, I was happy and when the time came I was able to use the equity in my home to start a business and purchase other properties.

My point is this, live within your means, get a home that is comfortable and in a neighborhood where you feel safe. Don't try to impress anyone, especially if they aren't contributing to your bottom line. Yes, I said it – if they aren't helping, your opinion is the only one that matters in the end. Remember -- this does not have to be your last home unless you want it to be. This is just the beginning.

END OF CHAPTER QUESTIONS

I want you to get some clarity on why you have started this journey so I ask that you write down answers to the following questions:

1. **Do you feel you deserve to own a home? If you are reading this the answer should automatically be YES. So, the real question is, why do you feel you are now ready to own a home?**

_____

_____

_____

_____

_____

_____

_____

_____

2. **How is your life going to change by owning a home? (Write down at least 2 - 5 reasons.)**

_____

_____

_____

_____

_____

_____

_____

_____

3. What was your biggest takeaway from this chapter?

_____

_____

_____

_____

_____

_____

_____

_____

_____

CHAPTER 3

The More Things Change,
The More "PI" Stays the Same

"Only I can change my life, no one can do it for me."

~ Carol Burnett

In my opinion, the most important benefit of home ownership is that once you buy a home and obtain a fixed rate mortgage, your mortgage payment, principal and interest only (P and I), remains the same for the course of the loan as long as you make your monthly mortgage payments on time. Since most people obtain a mortgage for 30 years, that means that your mortgage payment remains the same for 30 years or until it is paid off!

Let me put that into perspective for you. Rentals across the U.S. are at an all-time high and rising on average 3.2% per year.10 If you are paying $1000.00 a month in rent now at that rate of increase, in 5 years your $1000.00 rent will have turned into $1170.00 per month, in 15 years your rent would have increased to $1603.00 per month and in 30 years your rent would be $2572.00 per month!

---

[10] Abodo.com, *[REPORT] America's 2017 Rental Market in Review: Despite Renter Population Decrease, Prices Jumped 2.4%* Posted January 3, 2018.

Ain't it a PITI?

One of the terms you will hear referenced throughout your home buying process is P-I-T-I. PITI stands for Principal, Interest, Taxes, and Insurance, let's define each.

Principal

The original amount you borrow from the bank, and what you have to pay back to the lender. This number decreases over time as you make payments on the loan.

Interest

The amount the lender charges you for loaning you the money.

(Property) Taxes

Real estate taxes you pay to your local municipality to pay for schools, roads, police, public safety, and other municipal services.

Insurance

Homeowner's insurance protects you, your home, and your property in the event of a fire, theft or other damage.

Ladies, we are going to jump right into now, so let's take a look at Example A to see how PITI is applied.

Example A – PITI Breakdown

You purchased a home for $180,000 and your interest rate is 4.5%, your annual taxes are $2400 a year, and your insurance is $960 a year. Your total monthly mortgage payment is $1192.00. (You will divide the annual taxes and insurance payment by 12).

The $1192.00 per month payment represents payment for P-I-T-I
Your PITI payment breakdown may look something like this:

$ 912.00 (P&I) Monthly Principal & Interest (4.5% interest rate)
$ 200.00 (T) Taxes ($2400/12)
$ 80.00 (I) Insurance ($960/12)
$1192.00

Going back to our previous discussion of how PI stays the same, out of that $1192.00, $912.00 is the principal and interest payment. Guess what your principal and interest payment will be in 5 years? $912.00 a month! Guess what your principal and interest payment will be in 29 years? $912.00 per month! And guess what it will be in 30 years? $0.00, because it will be paid off!

It is important to clarify what can and usually does change annually is the **Interest (I) and Taxes (T)**.

In the loan documentation that you sign when you obtain a mortgage, you give your mortgage lender permission to collect the municipal taxes and homeowner's insurance payments from you monthly, (in Example A above it is the $200 and the $80), and remit payment to your city/county and insurance company as each becomes due.

Let's say you and your lender received a notification from your county that your property taxes will be increasing next year by $600. Using the figures in Example A, your property taxes (T) will be $3000.00 per year. Your PITI payment will now increase by $50 ($3000/12), and your new monthly payment will be $1242 per month:

$ 912.00 - (P& I) Monthly Principal & Interest
$ 250.00 - (T) Taxes ($3000/12)
$ 80.00 - (I) Insurance ($960/12)
$1242.00

Your mortgage lender has no control over what your local municipality will assess and charge for taxes; nor does your lender have control over what your insurance company will charge for insurance each year. Any annual increases these two entities impose will be adjusted annually by your mortgage lender and will be reflected in your monthly mortgage payment. These adjustments can cause your overall monthly payment to increase in the future so it's a good idea to plan and budget accordingly.

Amortization Schedule

To amortize means to gradually reduce or pay off a debt by making periodic payments on that debt. An Amortization Schedule is a schedule or table that shows the breakdown of the amount of principal and the amount of interest that you will pay towards the debt (loan) with each payment you make over the life of the loan. Below is an example of an Amortization schedule based on the figures used in the previous Example A.

Schedule A

	Total Payment	Interest	Principal	Balance
Month 1	$912.00	$675.00	$237.00	$179,763.00
Month 2	$912.00	$674.00	$238.00	$179,525.00
Month 3	$912.00	$673.00	$239.00	$179,286.00
Month 4	$912.00	$672.00	$240.00	$179,047.00

As Schedule A above shows, early on at the beginning of the loan the largest portion of your monthly payment goes toward interest. As you continue to pay on your loan, the amount that is paid towards interest decreases and the **amount** that is paid towards principal increases. Schedule B below, provides an illustration of the shift in the interest payment vs. the principal payment after you have been paid on the loan for twenty years.

Schedule B

	Total Payment	Interest	Principal	Balance
Month 240	$912.00	$330.00	$582.00	$87,419.00
Month 241	$912.00	$328.00	$584.00	$86,835.00
Month 242	$912.00	$326.00	$586.00	$86,249.00
Month 243	$912.00	$323.00	$589.00	$85,660.00

END OF CHAPTER QUESTION

What was your biggest takeaway from this chapter?

_____

_____

_____

_____

_____

_____

_____

_____

_____

CHAPTER 4

The Power of Equity

"Never allow a person to tell you no who doesn't have the power to say yes."

~ Eleanor Roosevelt

You have probably heard people talking about building wealth through real estate. The way that is done is through equity.

So what is Equity? Equity is best explained as the difference between the balance of all current mortgages and/or other liens and debts secured[11] by your home and how much your home is worth, or what the market says that you can sell it for at a particular point in time (i.e. market value.)

There are two ways to gain equity:

1. By making regular on-time payments and decreasing the principal (P) amount that you owe on the loan.

2. When the market value of the home increases.

---

[11] When you use and item as collateral for a debt the debt is said to be secured. An example of secured debt is home mortgage or a car loan.

Let's take a look at a couple of examples to further explain how equity works:

Example A

You purchased a four bedroom, two bath room, 2,000 square foot home in Port St. Lucie, Florida in 2011 and you paid $100,000.00 for the home at that time.

If you made a 5% down payment, or $5,000.00, your original mortgage amount would have been $95,000 ($100,000.00 - $5,000.000).

The $5,000.00 down payment represents the amount of equity that you had in the property at the time you purchased it.

In 2017, that same home had a market value of approximately $200,000.00. Now you would have had $105,000.00 in equity:

$200,000.00 (market value)
- $ 95,000.00 (mortgage amount)
$105,000.00

However, that $105,000.00 .00 assumes that you haven't paid down on the mortgage, which you would have done over the past six years.

Let's assume that you have paid $10,000.00 towards principal (P) on your mortgage over the past 6 years, because you have made your mortgage payments regularly and on time. You now owe only $85,000.00 ($95,000.00 - $10,000.00), on your home, which is worth $200,000.00. This would give you $115,000.00 in equity:

$200,000.00 (market value)
- $ 85,000.00 (equity)
$115,000.00

This equity exists partially because of the increase in value of the home, and partially because you have lowered the amount of the principal on the loan by making payments.

What could you do with that equity?

1. **Buy a new home** - Sell your current home, and buy a newer home. You could buy a larger home or downsize to a smaller home.

You will now have more money when you sell your current house to make a larger down payment to lower your monthly payment amount on your new home. Let's take a look at how this works with a real-life example in Example B below.

Example B

Last year you were promoted and you received a substantial raise of $1500 more a month in income. You have also outgrown your current home and you want to buy a new home with at least one more bedroom and another bathroom for guests.

Based on the previous example, your home is worth $200,000, and you owe $85,000. You now have $115,000 in equity which you can use towards the purchase of your new home once you sell the old one.

The new home you want to buy will cost you $225,000. With the $115,000.00 you can choose to make a $75,000.00 down payment and put $25,000.00 in your rainy-day fund. The remaining $15,000.00 can be kept on hand to pay your closing costs and other items for your new home. See Figure A below.

	Current House	**New House**
Purchase Price	$100,000.00	$225,000.00
Down Payment	$ 5,000.00	$ 75,000.00
Loan Amount	$ 95,000.00	$150,000.00
Monthly P&I Payment (based on 4.5% APR)	$ 481.00	$ 760.00

You are paying just $279 more a month in principal and interest for a larger home but you can more than afford it with your new raise because you have budgeted properly.

Please note that the illustration above does not take into consideration the costs associated with selling your prior home, such as real estate commissions, taxes, title, etc. The numbers used above are being used for educational purposes only.

2. **Fund your dreams** - You could use the equity to pay for education, or to fund a business venture. You would do this by obtaining a Home Equity Line of Credit (HELOC) whereby the bank would extend credit to you using your home and the equity in your home as collateral. Collateral is an item that is pledged as security for repayment of a loan (in this case your home), the item will be forfeited in the event the borrower defaults on a loan (i.e. via foreclosure).

When you use an item as collateral for a debt the debt is said to be secured. When collateral is not used, the debt is said to be unsecured. An example of secured debt is a home mortgage or a car loan. An example of unsecured debt is a credit card.

Notice I didn't say to use the equity in your home to pay off credit card debt. It is not recommended that you use debt that is secured by collateral, in this case your home, to pay off debt that is not secured by credit cards. Why? Because God forbid a tragedy strikes and you are unable to pay your debts. If you have unsecured debts the worse that can happen is your credit will be ruined for a while. But if you are unable to pay your secured debt you can lose your house, your car or any other items that are secured by the debt.

3. *Invest in additional real estate* - You could use the equity to buy some additional properties to start or add to your investment portfolio.

4. *Let it grow!* - You could do nothing and just know that you have that extra security for you and your family.

That is the power of EQUITY!

An Example of How Equity Builds Wealth

Mary was retired and working part time to make ends meet. Her husband passed away a few years before I met her. The one asset she had was her home. Because it was now just Mary living in the home, her home was too big for her. In addition to the size of the home, the maintenance on the land surrounding the home had gotten to be too much for her to keep up with; there was the pool to maintain and a large yard to keep landscaped. Mary's granddaughter called me because she was concerned about her grandmother having to work so hard on a job at her age to keep up with her bills and maintaining that large home. She wanted Mary to consider selling the home.

As it turned out Mary had a small mortgage on her home of about $25,000.00. The market value Mary's home was $275,000.00 so she had $250,000.00 in equity. Because of the equity that had built up in the home, when Mary's home was sold, she was able to pay off the mortgage, pay off her bills and, more importantly, Mary was able to purchase a beautiful newly renovated condo in an adult 55 and "better" (not older) community for cash. Even after doing that she still had over $100,000.00 to put in her bank account. Mary no longer HAD to work her part-time job. She continued to work because she loved the people, but she didn't HAVE to work to make ends meet. She cut down on her workload, had money in the bank, and could finally rest easy.

Loss of Equity

I would be remiss if I didn't discuss how the equity in a home can also decrease. With the last recession that began around 2008, home values dropped and as a result homeowners lost equity.

In order to illustrate what happens when you lose equity, let's look back at Example A. The house that sold in 2007 for $100,000.00 was purchased by the previous owner for $225,000.00 just four years prior. To keep things simple, let's just assume that the previous owner did not put any money down, that homeowner lost $125,000 in equity in 2007 ($225,000 - $100,000).

The owner still owed $225,000 to the bank that they borrowed the money from. Therefore, the homeowner was considered "upside down" in their mortgage, meaning the mortgage was greater than the market value of the home.

I'm not stating this information to scare you or deter you, quite the opposite, I want you to be aware that you can gain equity or you can lose equity.

Please keep in mind that equity is what I will call theoretical money, you don't have the money in your hand until you either:

1. **Sell your home;**

2. **Refinance your home; or**

3. **Take out some of the equity by obtaining a HELOC.**

I purchased several buildings when I was in my early thirties. Fortunately, I gained a lot of equity and I was able to sell them at a profit. This helped to fund my shoe business that I told you about earlier. It provided me with enough working capital and income so that I could quit my job and focus on my business full-time for at least a year without having to worry about having a job.

When I moved to Florida from NJ in 2006 I had initially gotten my real estate license because my then husband (now ex-husband) and I were investing in real estate and I thought having my real estate license would be useful as we looked for properties to invest in. Needless to say, we invested in some real estate that didn't turn out so well. Unfortunately, when the real estate market crashed, I not only lost all of the equity I had acquired in those properties but I also lost everything, including the real estate and my business. I was in the process of negotiating with investors to expand my business right before the market crashed and once the real estate and financial markets tanked happened, no one was investing in shoe businesses or any businesses for that matter.

Consequently, I had to start over and start rebuilding. But it was during this period when I was losing everything (including my marriage) that I began my real estate career. Everyone was telling me that it was the worst time in history to start a real estate career, Realtors® were leaving the industry in droves.

In fact, the energy around the office was all doom and gloom among the Realtors® that had lived through the booming real estate markets just months before, but for me I saw the opportunity to help people. This was a time in history when individuals were being preyed upon by scammers and unscrupulous people promising to "save their home" for a fee, and many of these scammers were successful because of the fear and uncertainty in the housing market at the time. I went on a personal crusade to help as many people as I could with honesty, integrity, empathy and compassion for what they were going through, because I had gone through it also.

With my prior legal experience, Wall Street and real estate background I became well known in my county for being able to successfully negotiate short sales and assist people in navigating the pre-foreclosure and foreclosure process. I understood the market, the terminology and how the banks operated. I personally negotiated hundreds of short sales for families and when it was time for those families to re-enter the market to buy another home again, they called me. If I hadn't been in the right place at the right time, which at the time didn't seem like the right time, I would not be here now with you writing this book. I thank God for that experience and all that I went through to bring me to where I am today.

Throughout it all I have learned some very important lessons when it comes to real estate and they are:

1. Stay within budget and don't over-extend yourself, purchase only you can afford. (Does this sound familiar from earlier?)

2. Do your research and don't be afraid to ask questions. Ultimately, you are the one that is responsible for the 30-year mortgage.

3. Although there are ups and downs in any market, real estate is still a great investment, as long as you follow rules 1 and 2.

In most parts of the country property values are not increasing at the rate they once were before the mortgage meltdown in 2008, and this a good thing, because the economy cannot sustain such increases. You should take into consideration where you live and/or will be buying your home because every market is different. However, in the long run, over 5 years, 10 years, and 20 years, historically real estate has been shown to be one of the best and safest investments for you and your family.

Test Your Knowledge

You purchased a home this year for $175,000.00 and you put down $10,000.00 when you purchased it. A year later you find out your home is worth $190,000.00. How much equity would you have in the home? [12]

a. $25,000.00

b. $15,000.00

c. $20,000.00

d. $10,000.00

---

[12] Answer: a.

END OF CHAPTER QUESTIONS

Write down 2 things that you would do 5 years from now when you have equity in your home:

_____

_____

_____

_____

_____

_____

_____

_____

_____

What was your biggest takeaway from this chapter?

_____

_____

_____

_____

_____

_____

_____

_____

_____

CHAPTER 5

What You Don't Know Can Hurt You – Understanding Real Estate Lingo

"Tell me and I forget. Teach me and I remember. Involve me and I learn."

~ Benjamin Franklin

Real Estate Lingo

There are thousands of real estate terms and unfortunately I cannot cover them all or this book would be as big as an encyclopedia (those of you who are around my age or older will understand that reference!). What I have done in this chapter is provide you with some of the most commonly used terms in order to give you a better understanding of the process. Don't try to memorize these now, although there is a little test at the end, but it's an open book test. Just read through them and become familiar with these terms. You can always come back to them for reference any time you need to.

I have grouped and divided the terms into four sections of relevance:

A. General Terms

B. Fees involved in Closing Your Loan

C. Types of Buyers

D. The Offer

Let's get started.

A. GENERAL TERMS

Borrower a/k/a Buyer - The individual(s) that is borrowing the money to purchase the home.

Seller – The individual(s) that is selling a home.

Realtor® - A Realtor® is licensed real estate salesperson that sells real estate on behalf of a Broker (see below). A Realtor® is a member of the National Association of Realtors® (NAR). Realtors® pay annual dues to NAR, and they have agreed to abide by a code of ethics established by NAR.

Real Estate Broker – Real estate brokers are Realtors® that have taken additional courses and paid additional fees to obtain a broker's license. Brokers may run their own real estate companies and manage other Realtors®. Some Realtors become brokers but choose to work under another broker, these individuals are called broker/associates.

Equity – Equity is the difference between the market value or the appraised value of your home and the mortgage (and other liens) owed on your home. (But all of you already knew this)..

Pre-qualification – In order to get pre-qualified for a mortgage you must provide the lender with an overall financial picture of your debts, income and assets. Based on the information you provide the lender can give you a general idea of the loan amount you qualify for. This is not a guarantee that you will be approved for the loan. At this stage, the lender will review your credit report, your credit score, and will run the information you provide to them through their system. They do not collect financial documents or verify any of the information that you provided, they are going only on your word at this stage.

Getting pre-qualified is great when you are just starting out or when you know you have some financial housekeeping to do to get things in order for your purchase down the road. It gives you an opportunity to talk to a lender just to see where you stand and what you need to work on. It can also help you figure out what your budget is for the house you will buy.

Pre-approval - *A pre-approval goes a step further than a pre-qualification.* Prior to getting preapproved you will send the lender copies of your paystubs, tax returns and other information to verify your ability to pay a mortgage. You will also authorize the lender to view your credit report and credit score. Your loan is then given an initial review by the lenders' underwriter, the underwriter makes the ultimate decision on whether or not your loan is approved, (the role of the underwriter will be discussed in detail in Chapter 7).

I will say this: if you are serious about purchasing a home and you know you are ready, go ahead and get pre-approved for a mortgage. This will cut down on the number of surprises and stress points down the road. Most Realtors® will require that you provide a copy of your pre-approval letter prior to or at your first meeting.

List Price – The list price is the seller's suggested sales price of the property when the property is placed on the market for sale.

Assessed Value - The assessed value is the value of the home that is assigned to the property by the property appraiser's office in the county or municipality where the home is located. The property appraiser uses a specific formula in order to determine the applicable property tax amount for the upcoming year.

Appraised Value – The appraised value is determined by a licensed individual property appraiser (not a municipal employee). This is an evaluation of the property's value at a given point in time in order to determine the property's market value. In most cases, the appraiser will evaluate similar homes in a similar neighborhood to determine value. An appraisal is required by the mortgage lender in order for a loan to be approved, and in most cases the buyer is responsible for paying the appraisal fee.

Market Value – The market value is determined by what a home will sell for, i.e., how much a seller is willing to sell the home for and how much a buyer is willing to pay for the home. Buyers and sellers determine and set the market value, and will often look to the current appraised value in order to make a determination of value.

Homestead Exemption – Many states offer Homestead Exemptions which may reduce the amount of property taxes you will pay for a primary residence. For example, if the property appraiser assesses your home at $125,000 and you qualify for a $25,000 exemption, you will only pay taxes on $100,000 of the assessed value of your home.

Every state is different. In Florida, in addition to the amount of the exemption, homeowners who file and qualify for the Homestead Exemption have the additional benefit of a 3%

maximum tax increase per year. What that means is that no matter how high taxes are raised in a particular year, if you live in Florida and you have a Homestead Exemption on your house, then the most your taxes will go up in any given year is 3%.

In some states, once you reach a certain age you no longer have to pay the portion of property taxes earmarked for schools. 27 states offer some form of a Homestead Exemption, so please check your state or county's property appraiser website for specific details.

Debt to Income Ratio a/k/a Back End Ratio - A mathematical formula that indicates what portion of a person's monthly income goes toward paying debts. This ratio is calculated by adding together all of the borrower's monthly debt payments and dividing the total by the borrower's monthly income.

Front End Ratio - A mathematical formula where the lender looks only at only the borrower's monthly mortgage payment and divides it by the borrower's income.

B. FEES INVOLVED IN CLOSING YOUR LOAN

Down Payment - This is the minimum amount of money that is required from you based on the type of loan you are receiving. You can always make a larger down payment, but the minimum requirement varies depending on the loan type. Some loans do not require a down payment, and some require that you put a substantial percentage down. Let's take a look at the various loans that are available:

Types of Loans

VA - **No down payment required** - The U.S. Dept. of Veterans Affairs (VA) offers this loan to military service members, veterans, and their spouses. This loan is guaranteed by the federal government. This means that the VA will reimburse the lender in the event that the borrower defaults on the loan.

USDA - **No down-payment required** - The U.S. Department of Agriculture (USDA) offers this loan to rural borrowers who have a steady low or modest income and they meet certain other income requirements. For more information, see https://eligibility.sc.egov.usda.gov/eligibility/welcomeAction.do

FHA - **Minimum 3.5% down-payment** - The Federal Housing Administration (FHA) offers loans available to all types of borrowers, not just first time homebuyers but you cannot have more than one FHA loan outstanding at a time. The government insures the lender against losses that might result from borrower default. (on a $100,000 loan amount you would be required to make a minimum down payment of $3500.00)

Conventional - **Minimum 3% - 25%** down-payment required. This loan is not insured or guaranteed by the government.

Private Mortgage Insurance (PMI) and Mortgage Insurance Premium (MIP)

Both PMI and MIP are insurance that a buyer pays for as part of her mortgage payment. This insurance protects the lender from losing money if the buyer defaults on the loan via foreclosure. So, although you (the borrower) are paying for the insurance premium each month, the lender is the actual beneficiary of the policy in case of default.

With both PMI and MIP, there are two fees. The first is an upfront fee like a down payment that is a percentage of your loan amount, this fee is included as part of your closing costs, which we will discuss below. The second fee is a monthly premium that is included in your monthly principal (P) payment. Now let's look at the difference between PMI and MIP:

PMI is required by the lender of a conventional mortgage when a borrower is making a down payment of less than 20%. The good news is the insurance policy and its premiums can be cancelled once you have achieved 80% equity in your home. You can notify the lender of this, or it will be automatically cancelled by the lender when your loan balance drops below a certain amount.

MIP is required by the lender of an FHA mortgage regardless of the amount of the down payment being made by the buyer. The price of mortgage insurance does go up if your down payment is 5% or less. Unlike PMI, MIP is permanent no matter how much equity you acquire in your home.

Closing Costs - All fees and transaction costs associated with your home purchase that are paid at the time of closing the real estate transaction. Fees that generally make up your closing costs include: lender fees, title insurance (discussed below), land survey, and certain items that are paid in advance such as taxes and insurance. Your lender will require you to pay in advance three to six months into your escrow account (for taxes (T) and insurance (I). A good rule of thumb is to set aside 4% - 5% of the loan amount for closing costs.

How does down payment and closing costs work in the real world?

Let's look at an example:

Example A – Down Payment & Closing Costs

You have been approved for a $100,000.00 FHA loan.

Your minimum down-payment would be 3.5% or $3,500.00

Your loan amount, the amount you would borrow from your lender, would then be reduced to $96,500 ($100,000 - $3,500).

Your closing costs would be approximately 4%[13] of $96,500.00 which is $3,860.00.

Your total amount for closing (including both down payment and closing costs) would be ($3500.00+ $3860.00) = $7,360 .00

Please remember to add an additional $1,000.00 to cover items such as your property appraisal and home inspection(s). The inspection and the appraisal is completed prior to closing. The total estimated amount of funds you will need to purchase your home is approximately $8,360.00.

---

[13] Closing cost percentages vary depending on your specific loan and your lender's fees. 4% is an average.

Seller Concessions, or Seller paid closing costs or Seller Contribution - When the buyer asks the seller to contribute (pay money) towards closing costs on the buyer's behalf. The buyer doesn't actually receive the funds in their hand, the funds transfer as part of the transaction; see Example B below for a scenario of how seller concessions may apply.

Example B – Seller Concessions

You make an offer on a home that is listed for $100,000.00

You offer $100,000.00 on the house but you ask the seller to contribute $3,000.00 towards your closing costs. In essence, you are really offering the seller $97,000.00, since $100,000.00 - $3,000.00 equals $97,000.00

Looking at the figures in Example A, your closing costs, without the seller's contribution, are $3,860.00

If the seller agrees to contribute the $3,000.00 that you asked for, your closing costs are now reduced to $860.00. ($3,860.00 original closing costs - $3,000.00 from the seller).

In Example A above, the total amount that you would now be responsible for bringing to closing, including both the down payment and closing costs, would be $4,360.00. $3,500.00 for the 3.5% down payment plus $860.00 for the closing costs.

Why would a seller agree to give seller concessions? Every seller wants to sell their home, for the most money they can obtain. The seller is ultimately concerned about how much money he/she is going to have in their pocket at the end of the transaction (what they will net, after all expenses are paid).

If the seller has in their mind that they will not take any offer less than $97,000, whether you make an offer of $97,000.00 or make an offer of $100,000.00 requesting $3,000.00 in closing costs, the seller will still end up with the same net amount at the end of the transaction.

I want to address two very important points here: First, by law a seller cannot contribute any money towards your down payment, the above only applies to closing costs.

Second, if the seller agrees to the $3,000.00, you are not going to get a check from the seller at closing, the $3,000 is going to show up as a line item on your ALTA closing statement[14] and that amount is going to be deducted from your overall amount due.

Asking for closing cost assistance from a Seller is a great way to reduce the amount of money you will have come out of pocket at closing; this will allow you to have extra funds you may need to make minor repairs or cosmetic changes. Talk to your Realtor® prior to making an offer, depending on your real

---

[14] The ALTA closing statement (previously know at the HUD) is the document that is prepared by the title company or closing attorney and it itemizes all of the fees related to the closing for both the buyer and the seller.

estate market if you require closing costs the offer you make to a seller may need to be close to the price that the seller is asking (the list price) and sometimes even above the list price if you are in an extremely competitive area. But your Realtor® will be able to advise you accordingly.

Please review examples A and B several times to make sure you have a good understanding of these principles. If you have any questions, please post them in the private Facebook Group: https://www.facebook.com/groups/BuyHomesNotShoes/

C. TYPES OF BUYERS

First Time Homebuyer - If you have never purchased a home before, you would obviously fall into the category of a first-time homebuyer. For the purposes of the government and its loan programs, however, if you have not owned a home within the last three years you may also be considered a first-time homebuyer. There are advantages to being labelled a first-time homebuyer because there are many programs available for first-time homebuyers. These programs include grants to assist you with your down payment and closing costs. Many of the programs impose income limits, so do your due diligence and ask your local Realtor® and/or mortgage lender what programs are available to you. Please take advantage of these programs if you qualify.

Owner Occupant/Primary Residence (Buyer) - If you are a first-time homebuyer and you want to take advantage of a first-time homebuyer program, you must also be an owner occupant. An owner occupant means that you plan to occupy or live in the home full-time, and the home will be your primary residence.

For example, let's say you have never purchased a home, and because you have great credit and a good job, your recently divorced sister asks you to buy a house for her and her children in your name for her family to live in. If you do that, although you are a first-time homebuyer, you will not be considered an owner occupant because you have no intention on living in the home yourself. You would not be legally eligible to qualify for first-time homebuyer benefits such as an FHA loan, or grants.

Second Home (Buyer) - When you own another home that you live in the majority of the year, six months or more out of the year; but you intend to spend some time in the new home and utilize it part of the year for you and your family. If this is the case, this home would be considered a second home for loan qualification purposes. This may be a vacation home or a home in a location in which you have a good deal of work or family obligations.

Investor (Buyer) - When you purchase real estate for the primary intention to rent it out to a tenant, or to fix it up and resell (flip) the home, you would be considered an investor.

D. THE OFFER

Comparative Market Analysis (CMA) - a/k/a Comparable Sales or "Comps" - A comparative market analysis is a report that is prepared by your Realtor® prior to you making an offer on a home, in order to determine if the Seller's list price is close to market value. A CMA compares homes that have similar attributes such as age, square footage, number of bedrooms and bathrooms, and that are located within a certain radius to the home you are considering purchasing. Request and review a copy of the CMA with your Realtor® prior to submitting an offer on a property.

Offer to Purchase (The Offer/Sales Contract) - The legal document whereby the buyer sets forth terms (such as purchase price, closing date, type of loan, etc.) to purchase the sellers property. This document is signed by the buyer and presented to the seller for acceptance.

Counteroffer – An offer made in response to another. Once you submit your offer to the seller, unless it is an offer for the full listing price, the seller will more than likely come back to you with a counteroffer. In addition to the price, the seller can counter offer other terms in the offer to purchase, such as the closing date, the inspection deadline date, or the amount of the escrow deposit.

Bilateral/Under Contract - The signed purchase and sale agreement between the Buyer and the Seller is a **bilateral** agreement once both parties sign. When everyone has agreed on terms and signed the agreement outlining those terms, you are now under contract and ready to move forward with purchasing your home.

Contingencies - When an offer has been made on a home and the Seller has accepted it, but certain criteria must be met by certain dates that have been set in the contract in order for the sale to be finalized. These criteria, or **contingencies**, typically fall under three major categories: appraisal, home inspection and mortgage approval.

For example, you may be under contract, but your loan must be approved in order for you to close, this is a loan approval contingency. If your loan is not approved by the loan approval deadline set forth in the contract you may have a right to cancel the contract and request the return of your escrow deposit (see definition below).

Escrow Deposit/Earnest Money Deposit - This is a deposit made by the Buyer to the Seller when submitting an offer or upon acceptance of an offer to purchase real estate. This shows the Buyer's good faith in the transaction. The earnest money is held jointly, on behalf of both the Buyer and the Seller, in a trust or escrow account.

Escrow Account – The word "escrow" means a third party holding something of value, temporarily, on behalf of the owner or owners, (in the case of a home purchase the "something" is money). There are two ways this term will be referred to in your real estate transaction.

a. Once your offer to purchase a home has been accepted by the Seller you will be required to make an escrow deposit to show good faith and to show your ability to purchase the home. The escrow deposit is held in an escrow account by a third party (like a title company, attorney, or real estate company) until closing. Once the closing takes place the title to the home is transferred to you, the buyer. The escrow deposit along with the additional monies for closing is transferred to the seller.

b. The money for taxes (T) and insurance (I) that you will make monthly to your lender is called your escrow payments. This money will accrue monthly and will be held in an account for your benefit with your lender. When your tax bill and insurance premium becomes due, your lender will make the payments on your behalf from the escrow account. This amount will change from year-to-year as your insurance premiums and tax rate changes as discussed previously.

E. THE PROCESS

Home Inspection - A home inspection is an examination of the property in order to determine the condition of the property. The inspection is generally performed by a licensed home inspector that has the appropriate certificates and training. The home inspector will examine the condition of the heating and air conditioning, plumbing, roof, attic, electrical systems, floors, windows, doors etc. The home inspection is not factored into your closing costs and must be paid for by the Buyer in advance. A home inspection is not required by your mortgage lender, however, it is highly recommended since it enables you to discover possible defects prior to purchasing the property.

Appraisal – A licensed real estate Appraiser is hired by your lender (but paid for by you) in order to determine the current market value of the property you are purchasing to ensure the property is worth, at a minimum, what you are paying for the property. If the property does not appraise you have three options:

1. The Buyer may request that the Seller lower the price to meet the appraised price, in this case the contract will be amended accordingly.

2. Buyer may be able to cancel the contract (if there is an appraisal contingency) if the Seller will not lower the price to meet the appraised value.

3. Buyer may move forward with the sale, but must bring in additional funds to the closing to cover the difference between the loan amount and the appraisal amount.

Although appraisals are very similar in nature to a CMA, mortgage lenders will only accept appraisals as evidence of a property's market value and not CMA's performed by Realtors®.

(Land) Survey- A land survey helps to protect your investment and is performed to reveal the boundaries of your property. A survey can reveal the exact property dimensions, location and size of the home on the property, as well as any other improvements on the land such as a fence or a shed that has been installed. A land survey is ordered a few days prior to your closing and is paid for by the Buyer.

Title Insurance - Title Insurance gives you verified assurance that the seller really owns the property and is free to sell it. Title insurance protects the buyer and the lender against any property loss or damage they might incur due to liens, fraud, errors, mistakes, unknown heirs or owners, or other defects in the title.

Title insurance differs from say car insurance because title insurance protects against events that happened in the past and the people that owned the property previously. This can be contrasted with car insurance which protects you against events that may happen in the future.

Homebuyers typically need two policies: an owner's policy which protects them, and a lender's policy, which safeguards the lender, the fees related to the title insurance are included in your closing costs.

Title Company/Closing Agent – A title company performs the research on a property prior to closing and ensures that the current owners (sellers) have the right to convey/sell the property and identifies any existing liens or encumbrances on the property. Prior to closing the title company ensures that all of the documents are in place from the lender and ready for the parties to sign. The title company also provides the parties with the title insurance policy. After the closing the title company disburses all of the funds to the parties, this includes paying off any existing liens or debts owed by the seller.

Depending on the state where you are purchasing the property, the closing agent can be a title insurance company or a law firm.

Closing Disclosure (CD) - The Closing Disclosure is the document that is provided to you by your Lender. It provides you with final details about the loan that you have chosen. The document outlines your monthly payment, loan terms, and fees associated with your loan. Your lender is required to provide this document to you at least three days prior to closing. This will allow you sufficient time to review and compare the fees that were initially provided to you by your lender and to ask any final questions that you may have prior to closing.

Closing Statement/Settlement Statement/ALTA (formerly known as a HUD-1) - This document is prepared by the title company or closing attorney and it itemizes all of the fees or expenses that are to be paid by the buyer and the seller related to the closing.

The "Closing" - The day when title/ownership of the property is transferred from the seller to the buyer. The day you purchase your home, Yay!!

TEST YOUR KNOWLEDGE

In this chapter, I have answered two of the most common questions that potential homebuyers often ask me when I meet them. Let's see how much you remember:

1. What is the difference between getting pre-approved by a lender and getting pre-qualified? *Write down which one you would recommend and why.*

_____

_____

_____

_____

_____

_____

_____

_____

_____

2. What is the difference between a down payment and closing costs?

_____

_____

_____

_____

_____

_____

_____

_____

_____

Below you will find real scenarios that you may encounter as you move forward towards purchasing your home. At the end of each question, enter the letter on the line that best corresponds with the correct answer.

1. You have $5000 to bring to closing to cover your closing costs, but your Lender says you will need $7000. If your Realtor® negotiates in the contract for the current owner of the property to contribute $2000, what would this would be called? _____	A. Appraiser
2. You would hire this professional to ensure that the mechanics (i.e. plumbing, electrical, etc.) of the house are operating as they should be. _____	B. Comparative Market Analysis
3. This professional is hired by your Lender to determine the value of the home. _____	C. Owner Occupant
4. If you plan to live in the home you purchase (and not rent the home) you are considered this. _____	D. Bilateral/Under Contract
5. You are just starting the process, but you know you need to work on your credit and save a little more money but you want to see what you may qualify for, you call your Lender and ask for this. _____	E. Seller Concessions
6. You have submitted your offer to the Seller. You and the Seller subsequently come to an agreement and you and the Seller both sign the contract you are now _____	F. Contingencies
7. Your Lender requires that you obtain this in order to protect against events that may have happened in the past to the property. _____	G. Home Inspector
8. You are ready to put in an offer on a home, but before you do you want to be sure that your offer is in line with similar properties that have sold recently in the area, you ask your Realtor® for this: _____	H. Pre-qualification Letter
9. Your offer has been accepted, but now you must complete your inspection, appraisal and obtain final mortgage approval, these three items are considered what? _____	I. Closing Disclosure
10. You will receive a copy of this document from your lender at least three days prior to closing. This document will outline your payment, loan terms and other relevant information. _____	J. Title Insurance

Answer Key: 1–E; 2-G; 3-A; 4-C; 5-H; 6-D; 7-J; 8-B; 9-F; 10-I

CHAPTER 6

There is Strength in Numbers!

"It always seems impossible until it's done"

~ Nelson Mandela

Now it's time to look at your personal financial situation and work with some numbers. Once you compete the exercises in this chapter, I believe you will feel a sense of accomplishment and empowerment because you will have a clearer understanding of where you stand from a credit and financial perspective.

Make sure you have your pencils sharpened and you are ready to go. In this chapter, we are going to discuss the following:

- Your credit & your credit score

- Qualifying income

- Your debt

- Your debt to income ratio

- Your budget

Before you read any further I want you to complete the following 4 tasks:

1. Go to www.freecreditscore.com and obtain a free copy of your FICO score and your Experian Credit Report.

2. Go to www.freeannualcreditreport.com and download just one of your free credit reports, other than Experian (you can download the other 2 later).

3. Gather your **paystubs** for the most recent 30 days and proof of any other sources of income.

4. Gather all of your **monthly bills** and put them to the side for the moment.

When you have completed all four of the above tasks come back here so you can move forward, I will wait for you!

Welcome back! Now that you have obtained and know your credit score, please write it down in Section A of Worksheet A at the end of this chapter, and then come back here and let's move forward.

A. YOUR CREDIT & YOUR CREDIT SCORE

Having good credit is more important than ever in this information age. You need to have good credit not only to have access to buying a home or obtaining a credit card, but in many cases, you also need good credit in order to obtain employment, car insurance, or to even rent a home.

Installment Credit vs. Revolving Credit

Installment credit is a loan where you pay back the same amount every month until the loan is paid in full. The loan amount is determined at the time you are approved for the loan. Car loans, mortgage loans, student and personal loans are all examples of installment credit. No matter how much you pay towards your monthly debt, your monthly payment amount will not decrease unless you refinance the total loan amount, the amount you owe will decrease as you continue to make your payments

Revolving Credit when issued you will have a limit imposed on the amount you are able to use or borrow, but you decide how much of that limit you want to use. Examples of revolving credit are credit cards and home equity lines of credit. You monthly payment will decrease as your balance decreases.

The Big 3 Reporting Agencies

There are 3 major credit reporting agencies: Experian, TransUnion & Equifax. Your lender will look at all three scores and will choose the middle score (not the highest or the lowest) to determine your credit score for lending purposes. Creditors[15] report at least monthly to the credit reporting agencies, but not each creditor reports to all three agencies so you may see discrepancies when you review all three credit reports.

What is a FICO Score?

There are several companies that provide credit scores using different scoring models. The most recognized company is the Fair Isaac Corporation whose scoring model is also known as the FICO score. Your FICO score is based on the data contained in your credit reports from the three reporting agencies mentioned above. When you apply for credit, the creditor wants to know whether you are a good risk or a bad risk. Your FICO score provides the creditor with information on how likely you are to repay your debt.

FICO Credit scores range from 300–850, the higher the score the better. Within this range there are five different categories ranging from very poor to exceptional credit:

---

[15] Creditors are people or entities to whom you owe money. While your Aunt Gladys, who lent you $1,000.00 to get your car fixed, can be considered a creditor, but she will not report to the credit agencies if you don't pay her back on time. On the other hand, your Visa card and the hospital where you had your surgery will report in if you don't pay them on time.

CHART - 4A

CATEGORY	SCORE RANGE
Exceptional	800 - 850
Very Good	740 - 799
Good	670 - 739
Fair	580 - 669
Very Poor	300 - 579

The scoring model that lenders use is different from the FICO scoring model, in my experience the lenders model is much more conservative and that means the score they use is usually lower than what you will see on when you check your FICO score on your own. So just be aware that when you check your own score and when your mortgage lender checks your score, there may be a difference.

Why Does Your Credit (FICO) Score Matter?

You may have heard people talk about how important it is to have a good credit score. You hear it on news shows, you hear it from financial gurus, but do you truly understand why your credit score really matters? Not only does your credit score give you access to the funds that you wish to borrow, but the best scores also give you access to less expensive credit, in the form of lower interest rates. Let me give you an example:

For the purpose of this example, let's say you applied for a 30-year fixed mortgage for $150,000.00 and your credit score is

685. The bank lends you the money with an interest rate of 3.913%, making your monthly mortgage payment $709.00.

Your friend Lynda also applied for the same loan, with the same lender, on the same day. Because Lynda's credit score is 630, Lynda's interest rate would be 5.103% with a monthly payment of $815.00 for the same amount of principal ($150,000.00).

Looking at Chart 4B below, you can see that Lynda would be paying $106 more a month. This adds up to Lynda paying over $35,000 more over the life of her loan than you would. This is one of the biggest reasons why your credit score is so important.

CHART - 4B

FICO SCORE	APR	MONTHLY PAYMENT	TOTAL INTEREST
760-785	3.514%	$675	$92,906
700-759	3.736%	$693	$99,654
680-699	3.913%	$709	$105,103
660-679	4.127%	$727	$111,774
640-659	4.557%	$765	$125,442
620-639	5.103%	$815	$143,292

Source: MyFico.com – Based on interest rates as of 9/22/17

5 Elements of a Credit Score

Your credit score is made up of five essential elements and each of these components represent a percentage of your overall score. These five elements are:

1. Payment history

2. Credit indebtedness

3. Length of credit history

4. Pursuit of new credit

5. Credit mix

To illustrate how each element works please take a look at Chart 4C below. In the last column, I provide advice on what you can do to help improve your credit, or, if you already have a great score, what you can do to keep it great.

CHART – 4C

% OF CREDIT SCORE	ELEMENT OF A FICO SCORE	WHAT DOES THIS MEAN?	WHAT CAN YOU DO?
35%	Payment History	Are you making your payments on time?	Make sure that your payments are never more than 30 days late. Payments can be 26 days late, but never 30 days late!!
30%	Credit Indebtedness	How much credit are you using on your revolving accounts and how much credit do you have available.	The lower your balance the better your score. If you have 2 credit cards with $2500 limit on each, or a total of $5000, try not to have an outstanding balance of more than $1500 or 30% (for both cards).
15%	Length of credit history	How long have you held your oldest credit card?	Don't close out credit accounts that you have had for years, even if you don't use the cards, keep them open. Creditors like to see that you have a history of handling credit.
10%	Pursuit of new credit	Creditors don't like to see too many accounts opened in a short period of time; it could mean you are having financial problems and looking to use credit cards to bail yourself out.	Don't give in to opening that credit card account in the store just to save 10% off that day.
10%	Credit mix	Have a mix of both revolving credit and Installment credit accounts.	If you have a student loan or a car loan you may consider applying for a credit card.

Exercise – Determine Your Credit Indebtedness

Let's see where you are with your credit indebtedness. This will give you a great roadmap on where you can start to improve your credit score.

1. Add up the **total** of all of your credit limits on just your *revolving credit accounts*: $_____

For example, if you have 3 credit cards with limits of $500.00, $2,500.00, and $4,000.00, you would write $7,000.00 as the total credit available to you.

2. Add up the total of what you currently **owe** on all of your *revolving accounts*: $_____

Let's use the three credit cards mentioned above as an example and say you owe, $250.00, $1200.00, and $3000 respectively on each card. You would add those figures and write $4,450.00 as the total.

3. Now divide B. into A and move the decimal over two spaces to see your total credit indebtedness: _____%

Using the numbers in the examples above it would look like this: $4,450.00 ÷ $7,000.00 = .6357 or 64% (I rounded it up from 63.57%.)

Now that you have learned to calculate your credit indebtedness. A simple rule of thumb that will help to improve your credit and keep it in the higher range is to try to stay below 30% of your credit limit on each of your revolving accounts (credit cards). Of course, you must also pay your creditors on time and manage the other elements that make up your credit score properly.

I hope that you have found this exercise valuable. I have personally done this to help me cut down and eliminate debt in order to improve and maintain my credit score.

Due Dates

Going back to Chart 4C, remember your payment history is weighed the most. It is the biggest factor in your credit score, so it is very, very, very important (did I say very?) to pay your bills "on time" each month. When I say "on time" I want to make a distinction between your "due date" on your billing statement and the "on time" payment that can impact your credit score. Let's now take a look at how this works with both credit card/installment loans and utility bills.

Credit Cards & Installment Loans

I remember going to Italy with my cousin and my aunt. We were driving with our tour guide, and everyone was speeding by us so fast it was as if we were only driving 10 miles an hour. I asked my tour guide, what's the speed limit here? He said in a cute Italian accent, "The speed limit is 50 but 50 is just a suggestion!"

Some experts may not agree with what I am about to tell you, but I think it is valuable information and it could make the difference between you not being approved for that house, (or a car or a job), or buying that house (or car or getting that new job.)

The way I look at it is the "due date" on your credit card statement, or installment loan is like a suggestion: that's when they would like to receive the payment. If they don't receive the payment by that due date they will penalize you with a late fee. Now, don't get me wrong: the late fee penalties of $20.00, $35.00, or $50.00 is money that could be used elsewhere, such as paying down the debt on that very credit card, or going toward savings for the down payment on your new home. But things happen and every now and then you just can't pay one or two of your bills by the due date, and you just have to incur that doggone late fee. That's ok, as long as it's only once in a blue moon (at the most) because remember: it's about saving money and paying off your debt, not giving your creditors more money in late fees.

Anyway, here's the good news! If you pay your bill(s) a few days later than the due date, or even a couple of weeks late it's ok from a credit reporting perspective. As long as your creditor receives payment on day 29 or before, it is not going to be reported late on your credit. Now technically I could have said day 30 or before, but I don't recommend that you pay it that close to the due date, because anything can happen. There could be system maintenance that day, it could get delayed in the mail, or the person in charge of processing your payment might be out sick. You just don't need to take that chance.

Utility Bills

For the most part utility companies do not report the on-time payments that you make to them to the credit bureaus, although there may be some exceptions. It is still important to make sure that your cable, water, electric and other bills (such as your cell phone bill) are paid on time because if they go into collections[16], the collection *may* be reported to the credit bureaus.

Here's a scenario for you to consider, it's the 20th of the month, you just got your paycheck and you paid all of your bills except for two. This month you had an unexpected car expense and can only pay one of the two bills right now. You have to choose between your credit card bill that was due on the 1st and your light bill that is due next week, before you get paid again the week after next. If you don't pay your credit card by the 30th, your credit report will reflect a 30-day late payment, you will pay a late payment penalty fee and your credit score will decrease. If you call the utility company and ask if you can make payment arrangements to pay the utility bill the following week and they agree to accept payment after it's due, the late payment will not reflect on your credit report so your credit score will not decrease, but you may be responsible for paying a late payment penalty, so be sure to ask, I would even suggest asking if they can waive the late penalty fee.

Another option may be to pay your credit card bill and then charge your light bill on your credit card. I want to be clear, these are not long term strategies that you should do every month because if this is happening it's time to look at your budget and spending to determine where you can and should cut back. I am talking one off situations and strategies that will enable you to continue to build and maintain your credit score in the event of an emergency.

---

[16] When something goes into collections, it means that the person or entity to whom you owe the money has hired a third party, like a collection agency, to get the money from you or file suit if you won't willingly pay it.

Lastly, remember try to have a good mix of credit. If you have a car payment, it may be a good idea to apply for a credit card also. After you get that credit card remember not to apply for any new credit unless you absolutely have to and to keep your balance below 30% of your credit limit.

When I say 'absolutely' I do not mean that you just 'absolutely' had to have that ridiculously expensive but gorgeous dress at Nordstrom for your cousin's wedding so you signed up for the card to save 10% that day.

Here is an example of what I mean when I say absolutely" – I recently had to choose between paying $5,000.00 for an "exploratory" repair on my 10-year-old car that was not guaranteed to fix the problem; or cutting my losses and going to buy another car. I choose the latter, because that $5,000.00 could have easily turned into a $7,500.00 problem or more, it was not worth it to me to take that risk on a 10-year-old car. As much as I hate buying cars (as you can tell by the age of my previous car: I won't even tell you how many miles I had on it!) this time I absolutely had to establish a new line of credit and buy another car.

B. QUALIFYING INCOME

Qualifying Income is your current monthly income that lenders look at when qualifying you for a loan. Not all of the income that you make may qualify. When lenders look at qualifying income they are not only looking at how much money you earn, but also how you earn your money. If you are able to document income from a part-time job or commission income or overtime pay for a period of two years or more then you may be able to count this towards your income in order to qualify for a loan. But if you received a one-time bonus, or an unusual amount of overtime a few times last year, the lender may not consider that as your income, since it may not happen again. Also, if you have a part-time job where you received payment in cash, the lender will not be able to use this as income. What's important to note is that a lender needs to see consistency and the lender also needs to be able to document and verify your income.

Qualifying Income can include:

- Full Time Employment
- Part Time Employment (if you have received it for two years or more)
- Bonus (if you have received it for two years or more)
- Interest & Dividends
- Social Security
- Child Support[17]
- Alimony

---

[17] If you receive income from child support or alimony each month add those, please make sure that you will be receiving this income for at least the next three years or more. If so, then add them to the worksheet. If not, do not include these figures.

Take a look at your paystubs. You should already have them gathered together from your very first exercise at the beginning of the chapter. Look at the last 30 days, or any other record of income that you receive on a regular basis.

Complete Worksheet A, Section B at the end of this chapter by filling in your income.

If you do not currently have the required sources of income, that's ok. At least now you know what you need to provide in order to qualify for a mortgage. You must wait until you are gainfully employed or can show income and then you can come back and complete this exercise.

C. DEBT

Let's now look at your debt, aka bills. Don't get too concerned about the fact that you have debt. It's ok to have debt, but as you know from the last section, first and foremost your debt must be paid on time. You also must have the income to support your current debt as well as the debt you want to acquire when purchasing a new home.

You have already gathered your current income. Now list the monthly payments for each of your monthly recurring bills on Worksheet A, section C at the end of this chapter. **This includes:**

- credit cards;
- car payment(s);
- personal loans;
- student loans; and
- alimony and/or child support.

Do not include:

- utility bills (water, electric, etc.);
- cell phone bills; and
- medical bills.

Remember you are only calculating your minimum monthly payment, not the total amount due. For instance, if you owe $2,500.00 on a credit card, but your minimum payment each month is $25.00, then just add the $25.00 to the worksheet, even if you pay more than the minimum each month.

D. DEBT TO INCOME RATIO

You have written down your income and your debt, now it's time to calculate your debt to income ratio. I have made it super easy for you, once you read and follow the instructions I have given you in the formula in Workbook A, section D, all you have to do is plug in the numbers.

As we mentioned in Chapter 5, your **Debt to Income Ratio a/k/a Back End Ratio** is a mathematical formula that indicates what percentage of a person's monthly income goes toward paying debts. This ratio is calculated by adding together all of the borrower's monthly debt payments and dividing the total by the borrower's monthly income.

In order to qualify for a loan, you will have to be at or below a certain ratio. For example, if you are applying for an FHA loan, your debt to income ratio cannot exceed 49.99% of your income.

Let's look at the example below and then we can input your information into Worksheet A.

Example A

Take your total monthly bills and divide them by your total monthly income to get your debt to income ratio. Then multiply that number by 100 to convert the number to a percentage.

Monthly Income
$3,500.00 - Gross pay from job
$ 500.00 - Child Support for next four years
$3,500.00 - Total monthly income

Monthly Debt

$ 250.00 - Car Loan

$ 150.00 - Credit Cards

$ 300.00 - Student Loans

$1200.00 – PITI (here you will give an estimate based what you feel comfortable paying each month)

$1900.00 – Total monthly debt

$1900.00 ÷ $3,500.00 x 100 = 54.29% debt to income ratio. (I rounded up from 54.285)

Let's say you wanted to improve your debt to income ratio and you only have three more car payments. If you can afford to pay off your car loan now and eliminate $250.00 per month in debt payments, your monthly debt will now decrease to $1,650 per month. This means that your debt to income ratio would improve and would now be 47.14%.

$1650.00 ÷ $3,500.00 x 100 = 47.14% debt to income ratio.

That means now only 47.14% of your monthly income is being used to pay your debt as opposed to 54.29% before you paid off your car loan.

Now calculate your own debt to income ratio on Worksheet A, Section D at the end of this chapter.

Finally, before we move on I wanted to give you an example of the current back-end ratios you need to have for each loan type:

- FHA - **49.99%** - your total debts cannot exceed 49.99% of your income. (some mortgage lenders offer exceptions based on your credit score)

- VA - Residual income based – your residual income should be $1,000.00 per month. This means you should have at least $1,000.00 left over each month after your debts are paid. It is ok to use the FHA back end ratio of 49.99% as a guideline.

- Conventional - **50%** - your total debt cannot exceed 50% of your income.

- USDA – 45% - your total debt cannot exceed 45% of your income.

WORKSHEET A

A. YOUR CREDIT SCORE

ENTER YOUR CREDIT SCORE	

B. TOTAL YOUR MONTHLY INCOME

ENTER YOUR TOTOAL MONTHLY INCOME	
Full-time and/or Part-Time Income	$
Bonus	$
Social Security	$
Child Support (court ordered)	$
Alimony (court ordered)	$
Interest/Dividends (from Investments)	$
TOTAL MONTHLY INCOME	$

C. TOTAL YOUR MONTHLY DEBT PAYMENTS (list minimum monthly payments only)

Car Payment	$
Student Loan	$
Credit Card	$
Credit Card	$
Credit Card	$
New Mortgage PITI (based on your budget)	$
Loan	$
Loan	$
Other	$
TOTAL MONTHLY DEBT PAYMENTS	$

D. CALCULATE YOUR DEBT TO INCOME RATIO

TOTAL DEBT	÷	TOTAL INCOME	X	100	=	BACK END RATIO
$	÷	$	X	100	=	

If your backend ratio is less than 49.99%, congratulations! You may qualify for an FHA mortgage. If your backend ratio is less than 50% you may qualify for a VA or Conventional mortgage.

Please remember that what we are doing here in these exercises are giving you an idea of where you stand financially, your mortgage lender is going to do a full analysis of your credit, income, debt and savings to determine if you qualify for a mortgage.

E. YOUR BUDGET

In this section I wanted you to begin to get a clear picture of where your money is being spent in order for you to determine: (1) where your money is going each month and; (2) what you feel comfortable paying for a mortgage each month.

Below is a list of items that many of us consume on a weekly basis, before we look at monthly expenses I would like for you to complete this Weekly Spending Sheet first. You will then be able to transfer these items to the Monthly Spending Budget sheet later.

To complete this exercise, for reference look at your credit card bills, debit card banking statements or if you spend cash start keeping receipts for the next couple of weeks and then come back and complete this exercise.

Start by listing what you spend weekly (on average) in the second column and then multiply that number by 4 to get your monthly total and write that in the applicable column.

WEEKLY SPENDING SHEET

EXPENSE	WEEKLY	MONTHLY
Groceries		
Dining Out: Coffee/Tea/Snacks		
Dining Out: Breakfast		
Dining Out: Lunch		
Dining Out: Dinner		
Entertainment (movies, shows, etc.)		
Nails		
Hair		
Transportation (Tolls/Uber/Bus/Train)		
Gas		
Child Care		
Dry cleaning/laundry		
Toiletries		
Other		
Other		
Other		

Just by completing this exercise, can you already see some places where you can cut back?

Now I would like to ask that you go to into the Resources section at www.tamaraceleste.com to download and print the "Monthly Spending Budget". Here you will be able to transfer the weekly budget items and also add your additional monthly spending items so that you have a complete picture of your finances and where your money is being spent.

Where can you cut back?

Look at your current expenses. You may grab a snack or a cup of coffee every day and spend $7 a day ($35 a week) when you can bring a snack from home. You may jump into an Uber to meet you friends twice a week when you can drive or hop on the bus. Or you can put some of your clothing in the gentle cycle or hand wash items that you have been dropping off at the drycleaner that don't require dry cleaning.

Now look at your budget and your current debts, what can you do within the next 90 days to improve your debt to income ratio in order to put you in a better position to qualify for the loan? Can you pay off a credit card or pay off your car?

Let's say you owe $1,000.00 on a credit card and your monthly payment is $100.00 a month. You also spend about $100.00 a week between eating out for lunch every day or meeting your friends after work once or twice a week. If you can cut back for just three months by taking your lunch to work and inviting your friends over for a glass of wine and a pot luck dinner, you could cut back what you have been spending on going out substantially. Instead of spending $100.00 a week, you may now only spend $25.00 a week. That's a $75 per week savings – multiplied out, that's $300.00 a month or $900 in three months. That's enough to pay off most of that credit card debt!

Below is a template for a 90-day plan. In the first column, I give an example of what your 90-day plan may look like. The next two columns are yours to fill in with your goals and plans. Be specific, but don't be unrealistic, as it will only discourage you. Limit yourself to just one or two goals within the next 90 days. Your goal may be to save $500.00, pay off one credit card, or improve your credit by 20 points. Write down specific action steps that will help you achieve your goals. Remember: this may mean that you will have to sacrifice a little in order to gain a lot. Write down what you are willing to temporarily do away with in order to save and eventually own a home of your own. Then answer the questions below the chart to help you think about your goals.

90 DAY PLAN

GOAL	GOAL	GOAL
Save $500	1.	2.
PRIORITY	**PRIORITY**	**PRIORITY**
1. Cut back on dining out	1.	1.
2. Cut back on spending	2.	2.
STRATEGIES	**STRATEGIES**	**STRATEGIES**
1. Grocery shop every weekend; plan & prepare meals on Sunday for the week	1.	1.
2. Sell items that I am not using on Ebay/Offer-Up etc. to earn extra cash to add to savings	2.	2.
3. Cancel subscriptions that I am not using, (i.e. gym, magazines, automatic billing)	3.	3.

END OF CHAPTER QUESTIONS

1. How do you feel about your total indebtedness? Were there any surprises? Is it higher or lower than you expected?

_____

_____

_____

_____

_____

_____

_____

2. What is your biggest takeaway from this chapter?

_____

_____

_____

_____

_____

_____

_____

CHAPTER 7

Gather Your Squad

"Alone we can do so little, together we can do so much."

--Helen Keller

Look how far we have come! You know where you stand financially, and you now know and understand some of the real estate jargon. Now it's time to gather your team -- your squad! Your squad is going to assist you with the purchase of your first home so don't take this part of the process lightly.

What Comes First?

Many people ask, "Should I get approved for a mortgage first or should I find my Realtor® first?" That question reminds me of the age-old question, *"What comes first, the chicken or the egg?"*

I'm going to let you in on a little secret: A good Realtor® is not going to take you out to look at homes without you first being pre-approved. So the answer to the question, "Should I get approved for a mortgage first or should I find my Realtor® first?" is this: it really doesn't matter. A good Realtor® will always be able to refer you to a good lender. If you happen to find the lender first, a good lender will be able to refer you to great Realtor®.

Some people have said to me: *I just want to look at homes to see what is on the market before I get approved for a mortgage.* You are absolutely free to do that. You can look at houses online, or stop by some open houses but if you call a Realtor® and ask her to show you homes she more than likely will not unless you have a preapproval letter in hand. You may find a new Realtor® straight out of real estate school that is an eager beaver that will be happy to have you in their car, but an experienced Realtor® will not. But don't take it personally and here's why: when you start home shopping without getting pre-approved you are doing yourself a disservice. You don't know much you are qualified for, so if you start looking at homes that are $250,000 and you subsequently find out that because of your debt to income ratios you qualify for an amount up to $200,000 you have wasted time looking at homes that were out of your price range. Additionally, you may find out during the pre-approval process that you only qualify for one type of loan and you need to save more money for down payment and closing costs and you need a few more months to save additional funds.

The analogy that I make with a Realtor® and a pre-approval letter is this: a pre-approval letter is to a Realtor® like an insurance card is to a doctor. (And no I'm not comparing a Realtor® to a doctor, I'm just to make a point). If you go see a doctor, they are not going to treat you until after they see a copy of your insurance card and they subsequently verify your insurance. To a Realtor®, your pre-approval letter is like an insurance card, it shows the Realtor® that you are a serious, willing and able buyer. People who are serious do what they have to do to get the process started, i.e. get pre-approved. Remember this is business, it's not personal!

A. YOUR REALTOR®

What is the difference between a Realtor® and a Real Estate Agent?

Many people think that anyone that is involved with selling homes is a Realtor®, I'm here to share with you that not all real estate agents are Realtors® and here is why. As previously mentioned, a Realtor® is a member of the National Association of Realtors® (NAR). Realtors® pay annual dues to NAR, and they have agreed to abide by a code of ethics established by NAR. The Realtor® code of ethics is comprised of 17 articles that cover various duties such as, a Realtors® duty to avoid exaggeration, misrepresentation or concealment of pertinent information pertaining to a transaction. Realtors® are held to higher standards, so since not all real estate agents are Realtors®, be sure to ask your real estate professional when you first meet him or her if they are in fact a Realtor® and a member of the National Association of Realtors®.

Why Do I Need A Realtor®?

You may ask yourself, "Why do I need a Realtor®? I can go online, find my own house and call the Realtor® who is advertising the house, right?" Wrong! When you retain the services of a Realtor®, your Realtor® works for you and with you. They know the real estate market and will negotiate the best deal possible on your behalf. Your Realtor® will know your budget, your house and neighborhood preferences, your likes and dislikes, they can help keep you grounded if and when emotions begin to take over, and more importantly your

Realtor® will have your best interest in mind throughout the home buying process.

Most people don't realize all of the services that a Realtor® does on their client's behalf. The Orlando Regional Realtor® Association published an article that lists more than 230 possible actions, research steps, procedures and processes that a Realtor® may provide in a typical residential real estate transaction[18]. Below is just a sample of some of the duties your Realtor® will perform on your behalf:

1. Search for homes based on the criteria you have provided.

2. Schedule showings

3. Review comparable sales

4. Prepare offers

5. Communicate with your mortgage lender to clarify mortgage terms and timelines for mortgage financing.

6. Negotiate counter-offers

7. Schedule home inspections

8. Attend the home inspection

9. Review the home inspection report

10. Schedule the appraisal

11. Review the appraisal report

12. Coordinate the closing with lender, title company, buyer and seller.

---

[18] Orlando Regional Realtor® Association, *The Critical Role of a REALTOR®® in the Real Estate Transaction, http://orlandoRealtors®.com/find-a-Realtor®/why-use-a-Realtor®/*

13. Prepare addenda or changes to the contract such as extension or credits.

14. Review closing figures to ensure accuracy

15. Coordinate final walk-through with buyers

And the list goes on...

How Does My Realtor® Get Paid?

I can't think of any other industry, other than the real estate industry, where the buyer of a product benefits the most from having their own representative and does not have to pay for that representation. In most instances, the seller pays the Realtor® commission. So even if you have your own Realtor®, the seller agrees to pay the Realtor® commission at the time of closing. How cool is that?

I would like to give an example of an instance where the buyer may end up paying their Realtors® commission. Let's say you find the perfect house online, but the house is a For Sale by Owner (FSBO). In many cases the FSBO seller will pay a buyer's agent a commission for bringing a buyer. But sometimes they may refuse to pay a commission and will want to deal directly with the buyer. As a first-time homebuyer, this is not a good idea. You won't have anyone looking out for your best interest so you need your own representation. You and your Realtor® could come up with a fee that works for both of you so that your Realtor® can represent you. You would pay your Realtor® a commission at closing as part of your closing costs.

How Do I Find a Realtor®?

When looking for a Realtor®, I recommend to start by asking for a "good" referral from your friends and family. When I say "good" referral, start out by asking someone you know that has recently bought or sold a home and find out if they were happy with their Realtor®. If so, call that Realtor® and start the dialog. Most of the great Realtors® out there rely on referrals. They value their current and past clients and they will look after the friends and family of those clients.

I just want to put this out there: don't feel pressured to work with your co-worker's, sister's, boyfriend's, little sister that just got her real estate license two weeks ago just because you feel bad and want to support her in her new career. Remember this is business and this is likely to be your largest purchase to date, so you want someone with proven professionalism and experience.

If you are unable to obtain a referral from a friend or family member or you don't care to share with your friends and family just yet that you are looking to purchase a home, there are a couple of other ways you can find a Realtor® such as:

1. Look at online reviews from Realtors® in your area on websites such as Zillow or Trulia. You can also view the number of transactions that the Realtor® has completed in the last 12 months on these websites.

2. Check and see if anyone in your social media circle is a Realtor® and send them a private message.

3. Visit Tamaraceleste.com and go to the "Find A Realtor" section. We are currently vetting Realtors® that specialize in working with first time homebuyer's. We will be adding approved Realtors® throughout the county to our list every month.

4. If you happen to start visiting open houses in the neighborhood where you are searching (which most people do), you will meet several Realtors®. If you bond with a Realtor® that you meet at an open house, follow-up with that Realtor® to see if there is real rapport and if you wish to pursue a working relationship.

Please note that if you decide to purchase the house at the open house that you visited, the Realtor® is also representing the seller. The Realtor® may not necessarily be obligated to look out for your best interest, so you should consider having your own Realtor®. This scenario gets into an area of real estate called agency, and every state has different laws regarding agency. In some states a Realtor® is not allowed to represent both the buyer and the seller, they must represent just the transaction where they have no duty of loyalty to either party. In other states they can only act as a single agent where if they represent you they do have a duty of loyalty, along with other duties. Just remember this, if you are looking at a home that and the Realtor® wants to represent the seller and you (the buyer) ask the Realtor® to explain their role to you under the law of agency. Remember you always have the option to bring in your on Realtor® if you feel uneasy.

Questions to Ask Your Potential Realtor®

In the chart below are a list of questions that you can ask a Realtor®.

Question	If the Answer is Yes	If the Answer is No
Are you a Realtor®?	Great! Proceed with asking the additional follow-up questions.	Find someone else, do not pass go, do not collect $200.00. (this is a reference from the game of Monopoly, for those of you who have no idea what I'm talking about.)
Are you a full-time Realtor®?	More time to dedicate to finding you a home and time is more flexible.	They may have less flexibility if they work another job. Ask follow-up questions about availability and compare to your schedule.
Have you been a Realtor® more than a year? (follow-up question: how many transactions do you close on average per year?)	May have more experience. Asking the follow-up question will provide you with greater insight as to the experience of the agent. A good rule of thumb for a more experienced agent (2 or more years in the business) is that they should be closing a minimum of 12 – 24 transactions a year (1 – 2 per month).	Length of time as a Realtor® should not necessarily disqualify the Realtor®, if the Realtor® is working with a partner or part of a team of more experienced agents that can help to guide them through the transaction it may be a benefit for you because you will have more people working on your behalf. Also, consider both the length of time and the number of transactions closed. A Realtor® could have closed 20 transactions in their first year, this shows they are a go-getter and have the transactional experience.
Will you provide me the name(s) and number(s) of one or two past clients that I can call for a reference? Note: If the Realtor® was referred to you by a trusted friend/family member you may not need to ask this question.	The fact that he/she responded affirmatively is a good sign. Call the reference(s), ask if the Realtor® was responsive, knowledgeable, professional and any other attributes that are important to you.	Not a good sign if no response, this should give you pause.
Is there anything else about you that you would want me to know when making my decision?	This open-ended question allows the Realtor® to brag a little about their accomplishments, but they should also address your needs, so listen carefully to their response.	If there is no elaboration here, you may want to consider looking for another agent. You are conducting an interview and this is the Realtor® chance to show you what they are made of and if they don't this could show a lack of confidence now and when it's time to negotiate.

Some Additional Questions You May Want to Consider Asking Are:

1. How long have you been selling real estate in the area where I am looking to purchase and can you recommend any comparable neighborhoods/areas in my price range?

2. How many first-time homebuyers have you worked with in the past year, or what percentage of your business consists of working with first-time homebuyers?

3. Are you aware of any first- time homebuyer grant or down payment assistance programs?

The list of questions above is not an exhaustive list, so feel free to add additional questions as they come to you or as you see fit.

Additional Considerations

Aside from asking the above questions, pay attention to how the Realtor® responds to you. Do some research on your own before making a final decision to commit yourself to that Realtor® (or any Realtor® for that matter.) Here are some additional things to consider:

- Does the Realtor® ask you any questions about YOU, or are they just trying to sell you a home? A Realtor® -- let me rephrase that -- a GOOD Realtor® will want to know about you. They want to know what your needs are, what your likes and dislikes are, what you hope to accomplish.

- Trust your gut. If you feel comfortable with the Realtor® that you have met, then go with him or her. You may have grown up in the same area, share a similar background, share the same hobbies, or have things in common that make you feel at ease. That's perfectly ok. Remember: we all want to do business with people that we like and feel comfortable with.

Real Estate Etiquette

If you are not in the real estate business or you have never worked with a Realtor® before, you may not know that there are certain rules of professional etiquette that should be followed once you have committed to working with your Realtor®.

- If you need to cancel your appointment or if you are running late, please call your Realtor® and let her know with as much advance notice as possible. Your Realtor® may have clients scheduled before or after your meeting and she will also need to reschedule or rearrange any appointments that have been scheduled for you to view homes.

- If you drive by or find a property online that is For Sale by Owner, do not contact the owner directly. Instead, provide your Realtor® with the address and contact information so your Realtor® can contact the sellers to obtain the details on the house. That is why you are working with a Realtor®, so that he/she can do all of the research on your behalf.

- Do not visit Open Houses or builders of new construction without letting your Realtor® know **before** you visit. That way, your Realtor® can go with you or at least call the

Realtor® of the Open House or the builder and let them know you are coming and that he or she represents you, if he or she is unable to accompany during the initial visit. If you happen to be driving by an Open House and decide to drop in, please let the Realtor® at the Open House know right away that you are already working with a Realtor®.

- Don't look at any houses with other Realtors® (even if it's just a friend.) Once the other Realtor® opens the door to show you the house they can possibly claim you as a client with regards to the house(s) that they showed you.

- If you feel that your Realtor® is not working out, let him or her know how you feel. Be specific, and give them a chance to rectify the situation. If for some reason it cannot be worked out, call and subsequently send an email in writing stating that you no longer wish to work with the Realtor®. This should be done *prior* to working with a new Realtor®. Also, do not look at houses with your new Realtor® that you previously saw with your old Realtor®, or your old Realtor® may be entitled to a commission. Start fresh and look at new homes.

- Be loyal to your Realtor®. Realtors® work harder than most people realize. They spend hours preparing for a meeting with you. They set up appointments, screen homes, meet with you, drive you to the homes, research comparable sales, and so much more. You are retaining the services of a person to work for you. You don't give them any money up front -- they only get paid if you find your home and purchase your home.

Imagine this: *You find this great new job and you are hired as an "employee." Your boss says, "Hey by the way, you will possibly get your paycheck in the next 30 – 90 days." You love your job and the people you work with so you don't think anything of it and you say, "Ok!" Then your boss says, "Hey, I need you to drive about an hour and a half each way to the other office twice a week." You ask, "Will gas be covered?" Your boss says, "No, but you will hopefully get your check within the next 30 – 60 days and that should make up for it." You say, "Ok, great!"*

90 days pass by. You are driving 3 hours a day two days a week and you work tirelessly and enthusiastically. On day 100 you say to your boss, "By the way I really love it here, but I see that the new girl Jane has only been working here a month and she has already gotten paid and I didn't." He says, "Oh yeah, I've been meaning to tell you we decided to only work with Jane. We only have room for one so we have to let you go, but you were great!"

The reality is that the above scenario wouldn't happen to you, but just imagine for a minute how you would feel if it actually did. Well this is how a Realtor® feels when a client they have been working with for weeks, and maybe even months' calls and says, "Hey, we bought a house we saw online". Or, "we stopped by an Open House that was For Sale by Owner and you were out of town so my co-worker's sister who has a real estate license showed us this house while you were away and we fell in love with it." (Insert punch in the gut here.)

It may seem like it's no big deal to you because you found the house of your dreams, but please put yourself in your Realtors® shoes. Just remember to be thoughtful. If you have decided the relationship is no longer working out, please have the conversation, no matter how difficult it may be, and let your Realtor® know so that you can both move on amicably.

The Buyer's Agreement

To prevent the above from happening many Realtors® will request that their clients sign a Buyer's Agreement. A Buyer's Agreement is a contract whereby the Realtor® agrees to assist the Buyer to find a house within their parameters, and the Buyer agrees to work with only that Realtor® until they have found their home or for some specified period of time. If by chance the Buyer finds a home on their own they will, in most cases, still be responsible for paying the Realtor® a commission. Generally, the Buyer will have the right to cancel with notice to the Realtor®, but please read the agreement so you are aware of all of the terms.

Final Suggestions

When you meet with your Realtor® bring them a copy of your pre-approval letter or email it to them in advance of your meeting.

Also, it is a good idea to become familiar with the sales contract that you will be signing. Even if you don't find a home immediately, at your first meeting ask your Realtor® for a blank copy of the contract and any addenda you will be signing in the future at your first meeting. This way you will have time to review the documents and ask questions prior to submitting an offer and signing the contract.

B. YOUR MORTGAGE LENDER

The mortgage representative (company) that you choose to work with is just as important, or, dare I say, even more important than the Realtor® you choose. Some Realtors® will disagree with me out of self-preservation. But the reason I say this is because your Realtor® can take you to find the house of your dreams, you can submit an offer, and the Seller can accept your offer – and everything seems like it is on track. However, if your mortgage lender did not do a thorough job (or if you were not truthful or did not provide all of the information requested) during the preapproval process you are not able to obtain a mortgage. And that house of your dreams will be just that -- "a dream" and never a reality.

Direct Lenders & Mortgage Brokers

Prior to getting pre-approved you must first decide if you will be obtaining your mortgage from a direct lender or a mortgage broker, there are pros and cons to each so you must find a lender that works best for you. Here is a brief explanation of each type:

Direct Lenders

Banks, nonbank lenders and mortgage banks are all considered direct lenders.

Banks – Banks are financial institutions that accept deposits and loans money. They do this in the form of several products such as savings and checking accounts, car loans, mortgage loans, CD's etc. Many people believe that getting pre-approved at the same place where they have an existing banking relationship will give you more leverage and improve their chance for obtaining a loan approval. This may be true in some instances when you have very good credit, low debt and good income (among other things). But because banks tend to be more conservative in their lending practices they tend to have stricter (less flexible) lending guidelines. If you are a buyer with a lower credit score, or you have other financial issues, a bank may not be the best place to apply for a mortgage loan unless the bank offers special programs or grants that fit your financial situation.

Nonbank and mortgage banks – Direct lenders that are not banks, can be smaller or mid-sized companies, investment banks, or a group of wealthy individuals that use their own funds to lend money directly to the consumer. Direct Lenders are more specialized than banks in that they typically only offer mortgage services and products, (and not the other banking products that I listed above). Direct lenders tend to set guidelines that are more flexible than banks and this flexibility allows them to be less rigid with their credit score and debt to income ratio requirements. Direct lenders also tend to be more solution oriented than banks when your financial situation is less than perfect.

Mortgage Brokers – Mortgage brokers act as intermediaries between the direct lenders and their customer, you the buyer. They do not work for a bank or a direct lender. Once the mortgage broker has gathered all your financial information they will "shop it around" to various lenders with the intention of obtaining the best rates and fees on your behalf. Mortgage brokers charge a fee for their service that can be paid either by you, the borrower, or by the lender that ultimately approves you for a mortgage, or a combination of both.

You will know, for obvious reasons when your lender is a bank, (Chase Bank, Bank of America, Wells Fargo, TD Bank, etc.), because you will likely have heard the name, driven by or walked into the bank branch. It may not necessarily be obvious to tell the difference when you are working with a non-bank lender or a mortgage broker, so if you are not sure ask your mortgage representative during your initial conversation if they are a mortgage broker of a direct lender (non-bank).

Pros and Cons

Now that you understand the difference between the various types of lenders in the marketplace please review a list of pros and cons for each lender type.

Mortgage Brokers

Pros

- Works with various lenders and can therefore obtain quotes from different lenders and can comparison shop the lowest mortgage rates and the lowest closing costs available on your behalf

- May provide access to loan products with lending guidelines that are less strict that may not be available from a bank or direct lender.

Cons

- May be partial to working with certain lenders and not inform you of all options available to you.

- Paid a fee based on the mortgage type, and in some cases, they may get paid a higher fee if your interest rate is higher.

- May not have a direct relationship with the loan underwriter (this term will be explained in the next section below) to address any issues that may arise, and as a result the loan may take longer to close.

- May have higher fees and higher costs associated with processing the loan.

Direct Lenders

Pros

- Nonbank lenders may have more flexible terms and a wider range of loan products to offer.

- May have lower fees and costs associated with processing the loan than a mortgage broker.

- Loan may close quicker due to a streamlined process, meaning the application, loan processing, and underwriting, all being done "in-house".

- May be easier to solve issues that may arise because the loan processing and underwriting is all done in-house.

Cons

- The representative for the direct lender Is employed by one bank or lender, so you will have to obtain interest rate quotes and fee information from each direct lender on your own.

- Limited only to products that the lender provides.

- If a bank, may have more stringent requirements.

Please know this, there is no wrong or right choice in the type of lender you choose, the choice is based on your own personal circumstances and preferences. In my career, I have worked with professionals from every type of lender, and I will say that my clients and I have had mostly great experiences with each type of lender, but unfortunately we have also had a few bad experiences with each type of lender. Ultimately it all comes down to the individual that you are working with at the company and their level of knowledge and professionalism.

I will offer you this additional tip; I find that the listing agent will often times recommend to the seller that the seller only consider pre-approval letters from lenders from their local community. Why? Because in the local real estate industry is small. Real estate professionals tend to do business with, or come in contact with, the same people over the years. They become familiar with individuals, their work ethic, their professionalism and more importantly whether or not they have a reputation of getting the transaction to closing. For instance, if the house you are looking for is located in Bowie, MD, but the preapproval letter is from a mortgage representative from

Newark, NJ, the agent and the seller may be a little skeptical. Not to say that your offer will automatically be declined, but if there is another offer on the table with a pre-approval letter from a lender located in Bowie, MD, this offer may be chosen because the seller prefers to work with a local lender.

Your Mortgage Squad

When you meet with and decide to work with your mortgage lender you are not just hiring that person, but you are hiring their entire team, below is a list of players on the team:

Mortgage Originator/Loan Representative – This is your first point of contact. The mortgage originator begins the loan process. The mortgage originator will document all of your initial information, such as your income, tax returns, credit score, etc. in order to get moving forward toward the goal of getting you approved for a mortgage. The mortgage originator will then send your loan package to the loan processor.

Loan Processor – This individual is responsible for processing and packaging all of the information received by the mortgage originator. The loan processor will typically input all of the information into the mortgage company's internal system. They check the file for accuracy and ensure that all of the information is complete and ready to go to the underwriter.

Loan/Mortgage Underwriter – The mortgage underwriter is a credit analyst that ultimately approves or denies your request for a loan. The mortgage underwriter's job is to determine if you are a good credit risk (or a bad credit risk). Think of them as investigators. Their job is to dig deep into your finances and assess the total risk by reviewing varying factors to determine your credit worthiness. They independently verify all the information that you provided and have several databases and tools at their disposal to identify fraud, ownership interests in real estate, businesses, and other information.

It's not fun, but it's necessary.

Be prepared to submit several documents throughout the entire loan process, which lasts several weeks. Some additional documents may be requested from you in order to verify documents that you previously submitted. You may be asked to re-send documents that were already sent in because the documents were not transmitted properly when you sent them via facsimile. This is normal, don't get upset. When your loan officer asks you to send a document that you know you sent two weeks ago, just smile to yourself and say, "It's on the way." When the underwriter requests verification of an extra deposit made into your account because you received a bonus last month, you will simply say "no problem."

Many people get upset and find the questions and information that the mortgage lender asks for to be intrusive and unnecessary. People get overwhelmed and just plain frustrated. Some equate this process to what feels like a 30-day colonoscopy. But it really isn't that bad, because you, my dear friends, will be prepared. You now know what to expect.

Since the mortgage meltdown in the early 2000's, lenders have become much stricter. They are lending money only to those people that they feel have the ability to repay the loan. What a novel concept!

Think about people that you may have loaned money to over the years and they never paid it back. If you hadn't been led by your emotions or your love of the person, and if you had really thought about whether they could pay you back (or done a little due diligence to see if they could) do you think you really would have loaned that person the money? Or maybe you could have asked for collateral (like a piece of jewelry, or a watch) to hold until they paid you back. When you are applying for a mortgage the lender is performing their due diligence to ensure your ability to repay the loan, but they also have the house for collateral just in case you don't.

What's required?

In order to get approved for a mortgage, at a minimum, your lender is going to require the following information from you, so be prepared:

- Most current pay stubs

- W-2's

- Bank account statements/Investment account statements

- Tax Returns (make sure you have filed your tax returns for the most recent 2 years)

The following additional information will be required If applicable:

- Divorce Decree

- Child Support Orders

Additionally, if you have experienced any of the following let your lender know during your initial conversation:

- Short Sale

- Foreclosure

- Bankruptcy

- Car Repossessions

- Divorce

- Separation

- Business Ownership Interests

- Child Support (payments or receipt)

- Alimony (payments or receipt)

Be honest with yourself and your mortgage lender. Don't try to hide anything that has to do with your job, your finances, or your savings (or lack thereof.) Trust me: they will find out. They may not find out in the initial application, but it will come out, and the unfortunate part is that it may come out **after** you have spent time and money on the home that you had hoped to purchase. You may have already completed the home inspection (and paid the home inspector), you may have even already completed the appraisal (and paid appraiser) so you could be out of $500.00, $700.00, $1,000.00, or more.

Below is an example of a real-life example when a Buyer didn't notify their lender in advance of a potential issue:

My client, I will call him David, was applying for a mortgage. He did like any normal person would do while applying for a mortgage: he gave all of his documents as requested, and everything was going fine and he received his pre-approval letter and subsequently found a home and went under contract. About two weeks into the loan process, his lender called and said, "You have a short sale that we saw as we were reviewing you prior tax returns." It didn't show up on his credit report so that's the reason it wasn't caught by the loan originator earlier in the process.

Unfortunately, the loan that David qualified for required him to wait three years after the completion of a short sale before he could quality for another mortgage. As it turned out, David finalized his short sale 2 years and 11 months prior (not quite three years). He was just four weeks' shy of the three-year waiting period to purchase another home. The problem was we were scheduled to close on his new home in two weeks. Thankfully, the sellers agreed to extend the closing date an additional four and a half weeks so we were able to close three years and one day after the short sale was finalized and everyone was happy.

But what if the Sellers didn't cooperate and the closing didn't happen? David's escrow deposit could have possibly been in jeopardy and he could have lost out on the house that he loved. If David had just informed his mortgage lender of this information up front any potential issues could have been avoided.

Questions to Ask Your Mortgage Representative

Are you a direct lender or a mortgage broker? See previous discussion on direct lenders vs. mortgage brokers.

How long have you been in the mortgage business? This will allow you to assess their level of experience.

What is your average time to close a loan? This will allow you to prepare and see if it corresponds to your timeline. Most loans should close within 30 – 45 days from the time you go under contract, and submit the contract and all of your loan documents to your lender.

What is the interest rate? Your interest rate is determined by your credit score, loan type, and length of loan, and there may be some additional factors. Be sure that if you are comparing interest rates with different lenders you take all of these factors into consideration to ensure that you are comparing apples to apples.

Is the mortgage rate fixed or is it an adjustable rate mortgage (ARM)? As a first-time home buyer you want a mortgage that is fixed, meaning that the rate stays the same for the life of the loan. The interest rate on an adjustable rate mortgage (ARM), will change/adjust at a set time every year, every five years, etc. and this could drastically increase your monthly mortgage payment, and therefore increase your monthly expenses.

Approximately what percentage can I expect to pay in total closing costs? Average closing costs run anywhere from 3.5% - 6% of the total loan amount. On a $100,000 loan your closing costs would be approximately $3,500.00 to $6,000.00.

Do you charge an origination fee and if so what is the percentage? An origination fee is a fee that may be charged by a lender for processing a new loan application. It is usually a percentage of the loan amount, and can also be called "points." This fee is typically added to the closing costs.

Many lenders with less strict credit requirements may charge an origination fee, so if you have some credit or income challenges and are unable to obtain a loan from another lender, the loan origination fee could be unavoidable. It may be worth paying this fee if it gives you access to the financing that you need.

What mortgage loans do I quality for, and what are the rates and fees? You may qualify for an FHA, Conventional, USDA or VA loan. If you qualify for more than one loan type, ask your lender to run numbers on all so that you can see the fees and benefits (or disadvantages) of each. One loan may have a slightly higher interest rate, but on the other loan you may not have mortgage insurance for the life of the loan which may save you money in the long term, so be sure to explore all of your options.

Can I lock in the rate? If so, when? Is there a cost and for how long can I lock in the rate? A rate lock is a guarantee from your mortgage lender that they will provide you with a certain interest rate, for a certain price, as long as the loan closes prior to the end of a certain time frame.

If you are under contract for a home at a time when rates are rising, you may have an opportunity to lock in the current interest rate prior to your closing date. That rate will be valid as long as you close within the time frame provided. For example, if interest rates have been rising every month for the past 3 months, from 4% to 4.25% to 4.50%, and you lock in your rate at 4.5%, if the interest rates continue to rise and it's 5% when you close on your home, you rate will be 4.5%. Your lender may charge you a fee for the rate lock. Also, depending on the lender if the interest rate decreases you may not receive the lower rate without paying a fee, so talk to your lender to get clarity on all fees and determine what is best for you.

Based on what I am approved for, what will be my monthly payment amount? This will allow you to see if the pre-approval amount falls into your budget. You may receive a preapproval amount for $300,000.00, and the monthly payment amount is $1,700.00 per month based on the preapproval amount. But if you wanted to stay under $1,500.00 per month your lender can suggest that you look for homes in the $225,000.00 - $250,000.00 price range in order to stay within your budget.

How much are you estimating for taxes and insurance each month based on my approved amount? Let's say the average taxes for the neighborhood you are looking in right now are between $2,400.00 and $4,800.00 per year. That's $200.00 - $400.00 per month. If your lender is estimating $4,800.00 per year in taxes, and the taxes for the home you love is on the lower end of that scale say $2,400.00, you will then have an overall lower monthly mortgage payment. The converse is also true, if your lender is estimating just $2,400.00 per month and the home you love has taxes of $4,800.00 per month, the taxes may take you over your budget even though the price of the house itself is within your budget.

What NOT to Do During the Approval Process

Many people are under the mistaken belief that once they have received their preapproval letter that they are golden, that it's a done deal. This is far from the truth. The truth is the lender will verify your income with your current employer, they will review your credit report and any other information that they feel is necessary up until the minute before you sign your closing documents. Try not do anything to jeopardize your loan approval, just be patient and wait to buy that new furniture after you have your keys to your new home in your hand.

Here is a list of some of the most frequent homebuyer DON'TS that may jeopardize a buyers loan:

Do not apply for any new credit or make large purchases such as a new car, appliances or furniture until after your closing. As I just mentioned, your lender will continually monitor your credit throughout the entire loan process. Any additional credit may keep you from obtaining a loan. If an emergency does come up where you may need to acquire additional credit, please talk to your lender first before doing anything.

Do not quit your current job or change careers. You may find your dream job right after you get preapproved for a loan. That's ok if it's in the same line of work, especially if it pays more. But your closing may be delayed if your lender needs to see paystubs from your new job. If your new position is not in the same line of work, the underwriter may think your new career is too much of a risk. What if you hate it and quit? Or what if you don't do well and they fire you? Communication is key: just talk to your lender first if you are planning to change careers during the process. If you just have to take that new job, it may be better to wait to apply for a loan.

Don't have large sums of money go out of your account or come into your account. You will have to document and verify any large deposits. This could delay your approval. For instance, if you sold a vehicle and received $5,000.00 cash that you deposited into your account, make sure you have a copy of the bill of sale, a copy of the check you received from the buyer, or other documentation to prove the transaction took place, and be prepared to provide this information to your lender.

This also includes accepting money as a gift from a family member for your down-payment. A family member can provide you with a gift for you to use towards your down payment and/or closing costs. But it really does have to be a gift and not a loan. .If this is your intent, you should notify your lender at the start of the process so that the proper documentation can be put in place in advance so that the underwriter is aware of the gift.

Title Companies & Attorneys

Depending on the state and even the county you are in, the closing agent, which can be a lawyer or a title company may be chosen by the buyer or the seller. Typically, the party paying for the owner's title policy will choose the closing agent. If you live in a state that requires an attorney for your closing and you don't know an attorney, then your Realtor® can assist you with finding one.

Is Your Real Estate Professional Right for You?

Whoever you decide to work with, here are some questions to ask yourself when you are meeting with and working with real estate professionals and deciding who will be a part of your squad throughout your real estate transaction:

1. Do they respond to your emails and/or phone calls in a timely manner? Don't get me wrong -- timely doesn't necessarily mean they call you back in 10 minutes every time. It may be a few hours because if they are good at what they do, they are busy with other clients. (Yes, it's true. I hate to break the news to you, but you are not their only client.) But if it takes a day or two to call you back, or if they don't respond at all, RUN NOW and save yourself from problems that could arise later.

2. Are they empathetic to your situation? Do they really want to help you as a first-time buyer or do they just want a commission? Trust me, you will be able to tell the difference.

3. Are they honest, or at least appear to be honest? You don't want someone that tells you what you want to hear. You want someone that is going to be honest with you. You want to know the truth about the housing market, you want them to be real about your chances of obtaining a loan, and you want them to be up front about the status of your transaction.

4. Do they explain things to you in "layman's" terms? You don't want someone that talks too fast and only uses

real estate lingo that you don't understand. The good news is that you WILL be able to understand what they are talking about after reading this book, but you get the point.

5. Are they patient? This is new for you, so any good professional will recognize this and will want to take the time and explain the process to you. They won't mind you asking lots of questions, and they also won't want you to rush into a decision.

Another point that I would like to mention and that I would like you to keep at the forefront when you are working with your lender, your Realtor®, your attorney, etc. is this: **they work for you, not the other way around**. Although you don't technically "pay" your Realtor® a fee, since as you learned your Realtor® gets paid by the Seller when you close on your home, your Realtor® does get paid when you buy the house. Without you they would not get paid. This also applies to your lender, and, if applicable, your attorney at closing; their fees they all receive are part of your closing fees.

Finally, please know that real estate professionals; Realtors®, lenders, lawyers, etc. get the majority of their business from referrals. So, if you are happy with the service you received please share your squad's information with your family and friends, they will greatly appreciate it.

END OF CHAPTER QUESTIONS

Do you know a mortgage representative or a Realtor®? If not, who will you find first and how?

_____

_____

_____

_____

_____

Why do you need a Realtor®?

_____

_____

_____

_____

_____

What is most important to you when looking for a Realtor®? (i.e., experience, qualities)?

_____

_____

_____

_____

_____

What are the three most important questions, for you personally, to ask a potential Realtor®?

_____

_____

_____

_____

What are the three most important questions, for you personally, to ask a potential Realtor®?

_____

_____

_____

_____

Name the three types of mortgage lenders?

_____

_____

_____

What are the three most important questions, for you personally, to ask a potential mortgage representative?

_____

_____

_____

_____

CHAPTER 8

There's No Place Like Home!

"We keep moving forward, opening new doors, and doing new things, because we're curious and curiosity keeps leading us down new paths."

-Walt Disney

Now we get to the fun part. It's time to find your home!! My advice to you: try to be as flexible as possible and keep an open mind throughout the process.

The search begins!

Neighborhood

Once you know the amount for which you have been preapproved one of the first things you must decide is where do you want to live. You can narrow this down several ways, by city, town or neighborhood.

Your determination of city, town or neighborhood may be based on one or a number of factors such as:

- School ratings

- Proximity to employer, family, etc.

- Price of homes

- Tax rate

- Crime statistics

Only you can determine these factors that are important to you, so please take some time and give this some real consideration.

Home Criteria

At a minimum, your Realtor® is going to need the following information in order to research and select properties that meet your needs:

- Price range

- Cities towns or neighborhoods where you want to live

- Type of home (single family, condo, townhouse)

- Minimum square footage

- Minimum number of bedrooms

- Minimum number of bathrooms

Please provide your Realtor® with as much information as possible about your criteria but try to avoid being too specific when it comes to cosmetic items like granite countertops or wood floors, for example. These are items that can be changed. If you get too specific in the beginning, you may inadvertently exclude homes that may have many other tangible features that you desire. Also, depending upon the Multiple Listing Service (MLS) [19] that the Realtor® in your area uses, sometimes items like carpet, granite, etc. may not be a searchable item.

Must Have vs. Like to Have

When beginning your home search, it is important to make the distinction between what you "must have" and what you "would like to have" in your home. For instance, you may have one child and you each need a bedroom, so a two-bedroom home is a must have. You may *want* to have an extra bedroom for guests, but do you really need it? Or would you just like to have it?

Here's another example, wood floors may be listed on your must have list, but ask yourself why it is a must have. Do you or a family member have a carpet related allergy? Or do you just not like the way carpet looks? If you found the perfect house in the perfect location but it had carpet, could you deal with the carpet for a few months or a year to allow time for you to budget for wood floors?

Think of it this way: A must have is a non-negotiable item, it is the absolute minimum you could work with. A like to have is something that is on your wish list, but if you don't have it in

---

[19] The Multiple Listing Service (MLS) was created as a way for Realtors® and brokers to advertise their client's properties for sale and offer compensation to other Realtors® for selling the property.

your first home that's ok. You will get it in the next home or you may be able to add it to your home later.

Below is an example of how you would compile your must have vs. your like to have lists. Immediately following you will list your items of choice.

Example:

Features	Must Have	Like to Have
Minimum square footage	1000	1500
Type	Townhome w/a garage	Single family (SF) home w/a garage
Outdoor Space	Covered/screened patio	Large Backyard

Now list yours:

Features	Must Have	Like to Have
Type (SF, condo, townhome)		
Minimum square footage		
Numbers of bedrooms		
Number of bathrooms		
Garage		
Flooring		
Outdoor Space		
Pool		
Homeowner's association		
On bus/train line		
Walking distance to shops/parks, etc.		
Other:		
Other:		

Home Ranking

When you set your appointment with your Realtor®, he or she may schedule you to see a half dozen or more homes in one day. You may not find your home on the first day, although I have several clients that fell in love with and purchased the first home that they viewed. To help you keep track of what you see and eliminate those homes that do not suit your needs I recommend that you rank them as you visit them.

When looking at homes, don't just look at the house itself. Observe the neighborhood when you drive into it. Does it feel like home to you? Does it feel welcoming? If there are neighbors outside, do they seem friendly? Give every home a chance, but if you walk in and absolutely hate it, it's ok. Your Realtor® won't mind you being honest it actually saves time and gets you to the next house a little quicker. Like I tell my clients: "I don't get offended. I didn't build the house."

If you really like a house, while you are there in the house take a few pictures to jog your memory when you get home. I also recommend taking a photo of the street number of the house as you enter or as you exit so that you remember which photos correspond with which house. If the house is occupied always ask for permission from the owner first before you start taking pictures.

Below is a house ranking sheet that you can use when you begin your physical search for your home. You can also download a copy of this Property Evaluation Sheet in the Resources section of TamaraCeleste.com.

Rank each category using 1 – 10 (with 1 being the lowest and 10 being the highest).

Property Address	Neighborhood	Layout of home	Condition of home	Overall rating
1234 Main St.	8	9	6	8

Do Your Research

If you are not completely familiar with a particular neighborhood, drive through the neighborhood in the morning, evening and on weekends to get a feel for the neighborhood at different times of the day and week. If you see neighbors, feel free to talk to them about the neighborhood. Just be weary of overly negative or positive people. Take what they say, bad or good, with a grain of salt, and do your own research.

Contact the police department and ask for crime statistics in the neighborhood where you have found a home. Your Realtor® is not legally allowed to discuss or quote crime statistics due to liability concerns and the unpredictability of crime.

Finally, a great resource that I recommend if you are moving into a new town or city is: http://www.city-data.com/ . This website will give you demographics and other information on your cities of interest.

HAPPY HOUSE HUNTING!

The Home Buying Process Summarized

We have covered a LOT of information thus far, but I thought it would be great to give you a quick review and summary of the home buying process for you to reference. Depending on the state you live in there may be some slight variation, but this is a general overview.

1. Obtain your mortgage pre-approval from your lender.

2. Schedule an appointment with your Realtor® to look at homes.

3. Decide on a home and submit an offer to the seller.

4. The seller accepts your offer and you go 'under contract.'

5. You submit your escrow/good faith deposit to the closing company/title company.

6. Your Realtor® will send a copy of the Contract to your lender and the title company/closing agent.

7. You find a home inspector and schedule and attend your home inspection.

8. Your mortgage lender will send you a loan application and a list of additional. documents. You must complete and sign the loan application and send in the documents as soon as possible, if you delay you may not close on time. If you don't hear from your mortgage lender within 24 hours of you going under contract you should contact him/her.

9. You receive the inspection results and discuss with your Realtor®. Here you will decide to: a) move forward; b) ask the seller to make repairs or provide a credit or a price reduction for the sales price of the house and you can have the repairs completed after closing; or c) cancel the contract within your inspection period deadline.

10. You will pay for the appraisal and your lender will place the order for your appraisal. You may wish to delay paying for

the appraisal until after the inspection if you think there may be an issue due to the age of the home or some other reason.

11. Once you have provided all of the documents and the appraisal results are in, your file will go to the underwriter who will review every single document, line by line, with a fine-toothed comb. This process will take anywhere from five to ten business days on average, depending on your lender.

12. The underwriter will request additional documents or ask for clarification on certain documents.

13. Your loan will be approved. (Or denied, but we are only thinking positive thoughts here!)

14. Your lender will issue a "clear to close" meaning the file is ready to be forwarded to the lenders closing department.

15. The closing company will schedule a time with you and the seller on the day of closing as indicated in the contract.

16. Your lender will send you a closing disclosure (CD) for you to review all your closing fees at least 3 days prior to closing.

17. You will wire your closing funds to the closing agent the day before or the morning of the closing, or if the closing agent will allow it, you may bring a cashier's check to closing. Generally, personal checks are not permitted.

18. You will perform a final walk-through the day of closing or the evening before closing to ensure that all of the items that were to remain in the home pursuant to the contract are there, and that the home is in the condition that you expected it to be pursuant to the contract.

19. You sign your closing documents and receive your keys.

20. It's time to go celebrate!

CHAPTER 9

Home Buying Hacks

"The secret of getting ahead is getting started"

~ Mark Twain

As we come to a close, I wanted to give you some additional advice and tips I call "Home Buying Hacks" to further help you along this journey. Read through them and take what you need, and disregard what you don't need at this moment in time knowing that you can always come back and review this section later.

Make an Extra Payment Each Year

This is my favorite tips to give to homebuyers. If you make one extra payment toward your principal each year, you will reduce your mortgage payment by six years and save thousands of dollars in interest.

For example, if you receive a bigger tax refund one year, take a portion of that refund and make that extra payment. Just be sure that if you mail the payment to your lender that you specify that the extra payment is to go towards principal or call your lender and explain what you would like to do and make the payment over the phone to ensure that it is credited properly.

Negotiating

I have seen many buyers lose out on the house of their dreams because of stubbornness only to regret it later. Let's say you have been approved for a loan at an interest rate of 5%. Not many people realize that the interest rate of 5% translates into this: for approximately every $1,000.00 in principal your payment will be increased (or decreased) by approximately $5.00. I say this because when you are negotiating, if you really love the house, don't lose a house over a couple of thousand dollars if it's in your budget.

For example, let's say you and the seller are at a crossroads. The seller has already come down $10,000.00 but you want them to come down another $2,000.00. If your interest rate is 5%, you are talking about an approximate $10.00 a month payment difference. (if your interest rate is 4.5% you are talking approximately $9.00 a month) If you won't increase your offer to $2,000.00 to meet a Seller, you may miss out on a house that would have only cost you $10 more a month or $120.00 more a year. Ask yourself, Is it really worth it?

Shopping Days

I recommend that you designate Tuesday, Wednesday and/or Thursday to look at homes, especially if you reside in a highly competitive real estate market. If you find a home that you love I also recommend submitting your offer by Thursday and have your Realtor® request that the Seller(s) respond by Friday. This will allow you to beat the weekend rush, when everyone is out looking at homes on Saturday and Sunday, in my experience this gives you a competitive advantage when submitting offers.

Home Inspection

A home inspection is not mandatory and generally it is not required by your lender. However, do not forgo the home inspection in order to save a couple of hundred dollars. An example of what could happen when you don't have a home inspection is this: you close on the house, then move in and find out that when it rains the roof leaks. Now it's your house and you must spend $10,000.00 on a new roof. If you had performed a home inspection, this may have been detected and you could have 1.) asked the sellers to pay for the roof; 2.) asked the sellers to reduce the price by the replacement costs for the roof, or 3.) cancelled the contract within your inspection period.

Age of Roof

Always ask how old the roof is. If the roof is over 15 – 25 years old. depending on where you reside, the house may not be insurable. The official insurance term is that the roof is at the end of its "useful life." Once you find out the age of the roof, especially if it is up there in age, call you insurance agent ASAP to see if this will be any potential problems insuring the house due to the age of the roof.

Homeowner's Insurance

Speaking of Insurance, your lender may offer to provide you with insurance quotes, but in order to ensure that you are receiving the best rate possible I recommend that you call various insurance companies on your own behalf. Start by calling your current insurance company that has your car insurance. You may save by bundling the car and homeowner's insurance together.

Home Warranty Protection Plan

A home warranty protection plan is tantamount to having an insurance policy for certain features of your house such as, the air conditioning and heating unit, appliances, water heater and depending on your policy, it may also cover some small electrical and plumbing issues.

I believe a home warranty protection plan is the best way to help you budget for large expenses. For example, let's say the appliances or the central air unit in the house are older, and therefore are likely to need repairs in the near future. You can purchase a home warranty protection plan and it can cover service calls, or, if the item needs to be replaced entirely it may be covered depending on your policy. These plans vary, but on average cost around $500.00 per year. You may also consider adding this request into your offer and asking the seller to pay for the first year of the warranty.

Renter's Insurance

This one is not really a home buying tip, but I think that it is worthwhile mentioning. While you are currently renting, please make sure you obtain renter's insurance to ensure that your belongings are covered in the event of fire, flood or theft. For $20.00 - $30.00 a month, it's definitely worth it!

Resale

Although you are just getting started as a new homeowner think toward the future when buying your home. Ask yourself what are some of the features that would make it attractive to someone else when you sell the home (resell). For instance, if you are looking at a home on a main road that has a lot of traffic, you may have some difficulty selling it at a price that similar homes are selling for later on that are not on a busy road. If you only have one bathroom that may also cause a resale issue later so you may want to look at a home with two bathrooms, if it is within your price range.

Property Taxes and Millage Rate

Do some research ahead of time on how much taxes are in your desired neighborhood. For instance, do a Google search for "Property Tax Millage Rate for (Insert your city and state)." Remember property taxes are based on assessed value and not the market value, which is a good thing. Assessed value is generally less than market value because the property appraiser is usually a year behind in assessing property values and have not caught up to the current market.

The millage rate works is like this: if your millage rate is 25, that means your property tax is calculated at a rate of $25 for every $1,000.00 of the assessed value of the home. Another way to calculate it is to take 2.5% mils per $1,000.00 of home value.

For example, on a $100,000 home with a millage rate of 25, the taxes would be $2,500.00 ($100,000.00 x .025.)

Budget

Depending on the state, city, or county where you live, the current tax rate for the previous buyer may not be you tax rate once the property is assessed for the new year. It may increase with the transfer of ownership. Your Realtor® can help you determine this or you can call your local property appraisers office directly. Just be sure your budget allows for a possible increase in your escrow account for the following year. Also, budget for incidentals and things that will break down in the house -- remember you are now your own landlord! There is no one to call but a plumber when the sink gets clogged and you now have to pay for it.

Homeowner & Condominium Associations

There are pros and cons to living in a home that is governed by an association.

One of the main pros is that everyone has to follow the same rules or there will be penalties imposed upon those that do not conform. The rules are there to maintain uniformity (your neighbor will not be able to paint their house purple for example) and helps to maintain the values of the homes in the community or building.

A con is that often the associations can have restrictions that do not work with your lifestyle. For instance, some may not allow trucks or motorcycles. If you like to garden, there may be restrictions on what is allowed to be planted. Also, if you have pets or plan on getting a pet, some associations may restrict the number and type of pets that you may have in your home.

Finally, depending on your particular circumstance the following can be seen as either a pro or a con: the association may have minimum credit score requirements or may require all residents to have a criminal background check. I recently had clients that were very interested in purchasing a home in a gated community, but their son had gotten into some trouble and was getting out of prison soon. They were concerned that when he came to live with him he may not be approved by the association to live there. This was a legitimate concern and we delayed putting in the offer so that they could evaluate and determine what was best for their family.

If you are considering purchasing a condominium or a home that is governed by an association, please be sure that you and your Realtor® read the rules and regulations of the association and all other applicable governing documents prior to submitting your offer.

Time frames

If you are currently renting and your lease is up in six months, and you have a great financial picture so you don't believe that you would have a problem getting approved for a mortgage, you may want to start the mortgage process and start looking for a home approximately three months before your lease expires.

If you have some financial challenges, you may want to consider starting the process up to 12 months before your lease expires in order to give you a chance to rectify any issues that crop up. Every real estate market is different so these time frames are just suggestions, you should talk to the real estate professionals in your area to determine when is the right time for you to begin the process.

Be responsive

Please respond to your lender immediately when they request additional information. Also, you may have to sign additional paperwork that your Realtor® (or lender) provides to you throughout the process. In many cases, if you take several days to respond, our file will now be under a pile of other files that are sitting on the lender's desk and it may now take your lender a couple of days to get back to your file. If you respond right away to a question or document that an underwriter asks for, the underwriter may be able to go right back into the file and resolve the issue without delay.

Cash Is Not King All the Time

Many people don't believe in using credit, writing checks or keeping their money in a bank account, they do everything in cash. Unfortunately, lenders feel the opposite. Lenders need to see a pattern. They need to see the pay pattern, that you receive a paycheck, and they also need to see the payment pattern, that you pay rent and other bills regularly. This shows that you are responsible and can pay all of your obligations each month.

If you cash your checks at a check cashing store, and pay all of your bills in cash, then the next time you get paid, go and open a bank account and start paying your bills through that account.

Let's say you live with a relative: mom, dad, sister, etc., and you give them money every month for rent, but you give them cash. From this moment forward write them a check or at the very least give them a money order until you can establish your checking account, and keep a copy of the money order.

File your taxes

If you have not yet filed your taxes for the most current year, do so online or stop at your nearest tax preparation establishment and get that started today prior to meeting with your lender!

Investment Properties

I promised to address the issue if you happen to reside in a city where the price to purchase a home is extremely high, such as cities like San Francisco, New York, or Seattle. If you are able, I would like you to consider purchasing a property that is less expensive as investment property just to get into the market. Maybe it's in a city where you grew up, or where you have family members that you can trust to keep an eye on the property. When I purchased my investment property, I was living in New Jersey but I purchased property in Connecticut where I grew up because I was able to get better deals, and I hired my brother as my property manager. Start with a small condo that will not have a lot of maintenance and rent it out. It's something to consider.

Please join and reach out to me in the private Facebook group: https://www.facebook.com/groups/BuyHomesNotShoes/ and I will be happy to work with you to achieve this goal.

I truly hope that this book has added value to your home buying experience. You should now feel informed and empowered to go out and find the home of your dreams. Remember to have a positive attitude and keep an open mind and you will be just fine!

Now -- go forth and prosper!

Xoxo
Tamara Celeste

Acknowledgements

I would like to thank my mother Teri, my brother James and my step-dad Al for always supporting me no matter what I decided to embark upon. I want to thank Derek for being my "DP", my Gibraltar and for keeping me grounded. I want to thank my past clients that I have had the pleasure to work with over the years. Because of all of you I gained the knowledge and experience that has allowed me to succeed in this business and to write this book.

To: Jahkaree, Alyssa, Raena, Jayda, Sasha, Aaliyah, Mackenzie, Davey, Alexa, Grant, & LJ, remember to stay true to who you are, always set goals and reach for the stars, you can achieve whatever you set your mind to.

I would also like to thank Javier I. and Carol D. for taking time to talk "mortgage talk" with me. Finally, Michelle K. thank your patience, support and guidance throughout this entire process, you are truly the best!!

About the Author

Tamara Celeste, the Home Buying Coach is a lawyer, real estate broker, entrepreneur, coach and author. Tamara is passionate about speaking, teaching and encouraging women to become homeowners and/or investors.

If you are interested in having Tamara speak or hold a workshop for your group or organization, please visit

TamaraCeleste.com.

Connect with Tamara

FACEBOOK:

https://www.facebook.com/groups/BuyHomesNotShoes/

LINKEDIN:

https://www.linkedin.com/in/tamaraceleste/

WEBSITE:

www.tamaraceleste.com

Can You Do Me a Huge Favor?

I hope you've enjoyed this book because I enjoyed writing it for you!

I would greatly appreciate your honest review on Amazon for this book. To write a review go to Amazon and select this book and write your glowing review!

Getting reviews is not so easy these days, but they help the author immensely!

So, if you could find it in your heart to go write a review, I will be eternally grateful!

Made in the USA
Middletown, DE
14 July 2020

12802551R00096